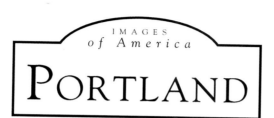

IMAGES
of America

PORTLAND

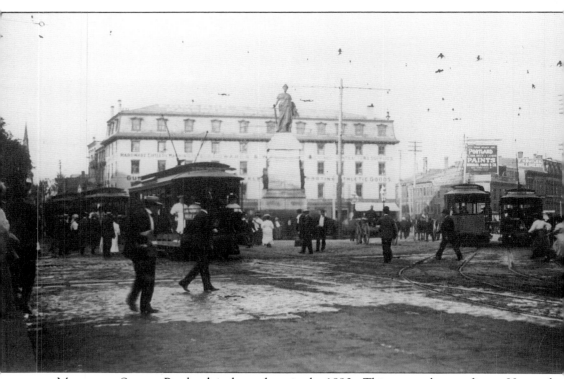

Monument Square, Portland, is shown here in the 1890s. This square, known first as Haymarke Square, has been a hub of Portland activity for more than two centuries.

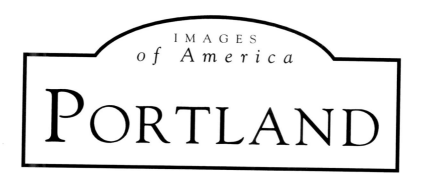

IMAGES
of America

PORTLAND

By Frank H. Sleeper
From the Maine Historic Preservation Commission
and Others

ARCADIA
PUBLISHING

Published by Arcadia Publishing
Charleston, South Carolina

Printed in the United States of America

Library of Congress Catalog Card Number: Applied for

For all general information contact Arcadia Publishing at:
Telephone 843-853-2070
Fax 843-853-0044
E-mail sales@arcadiapublishing.com
For customer service and orders:
Toll-Free 1-888-313-2665

Visit us on the Internet at www.arcadiapublishing.com

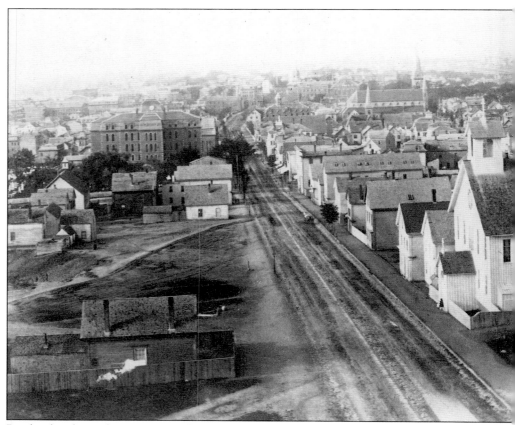

Portland is shown here in a view from Munjoy Hill in the 1870s. Munjoy Hill was named afte
George Munjoy, the son-in-law of George Cleeves, one of the city's founders. Munjoy moved t
the Neck in 1689 and had cow-grazing rights on 3 acres of land on the hill.

Contents

Introduction 7

1. The Phoenix Factor 9

2. Phoenix Expanded 15

3. The Jewish Community 35

4. Doers and Shakers 53

5. The Waterfront 69

6. Leisure and Sports 85

7. Congress Street 109

Acknowledgments 128

Introduction

Maine's largest city has been known through its history as an example of the mythological phoenix, the animal that rises again out of the ashes of its apparent death. Portland, originally called Falmouth, did so several times early in its history: during the French and Indian Wars it was destroyed twice (in 1676 and 1690), and on October 18, 1775, it was burned by Captain Mowatt of the British Navy. After each disaster, the city was rebuilt and continued on. But the worst was yet to come: on July 4, 1866, the most devastating fire in the city's history destroyed 1,500 homes and businesses, leaving 10,000 people homeless. Yet, despite the magnitude of the disaster, Portland rose again from the ashes.

In this book, I have expanded the phoenix theme to include those who have come to Portland from overseas, fleeing from economic disasters (like the Irish potato famine) or from political or religious oppression. Portland's Jewish community, the largest in the state, came from the pogroms and discrimination of Eastern Europe under the Russian Czars. Immigrants from all over the world have literally risen out of the ashes, and emerged into Portland.

The emergence of Portland's immigrants was felt economically and politically. Their drive, determination, and relentless pursuit of a better life fueled many of Portland's business activities. Their most obvious political victories came in the mid-1950s, after the Democratic gubernatorial victory of Edmund S. Muskie in 1954.

Rising from the ashes, economically, politically, socially, and otherwise, requires a solid base, at least in the nineteenth and twentieth centuries. That base was supplied by several Portland families, long-established in the community, some even directly descended from the first settlers of Falmouth. These families had a spirit of public commitment that served the whole community well.

Portland's waterfront was a place where many of those coming out of the ashes of foreign countries found work. But it also had its own phoenix-like history. It was, of course, hit hard by the embargo in the early 1800s. With the construction of railroads to the north and west, Portland became the ice-free winter port for eastern and central Canada. That distinction was lost about 1920 when Canadian policy changed and Halifax and Saint John were promoted to take Portland's place. The grain elevators eventually came down. The China clay no longer appeared. The oil that came and went to Montreal over the Portland Pipe Line ended up in South Portland, shifting the waterfront a bit. Business along the waterfront fell off badly, but it eventually turned the corner and came back to some degree.

The phoenix factor is again apparent when one considers the history of what used to be Portland's and probably Maine's busiest business street, Congress Street. Congress Street lost its business hub status, especially on the retail side, after the establishment of the giant Maine Mall Shopping Center in neighboring South Portland. But it's not dead. Between its growth as a cultural center (in spite of the difficulties faced by the State Theater) and the efforts of Elizabeth Noyce, Congress Street appears likely to be on the rise again. But this rise from the ashes has involved a near-constant struggle.

One consistent theme among the five Maine communities that I've written books on, from Presque Isle and Caribou down to Portland, is that much of Maine life is struggle—and that Maine people, whatever else they may not have, have an abundance of what is generally referred to as "guts." They need to have that quality to survive in this state. That's true both of people who were born and raised in Maine and people who come here to live permanently. Among other ingredients, this form of guts includes persistence and the ability to adapt to change. These are qualities devoutly to be wished for, but they are almost a necessity for long-term survival in Maine.

Portland's waterfront has shown this brand of guts over the years. But Portland also has a lighter side. People made good use of what leisure time they had, and the area has a very strong sports tradition. As the largest city in the state, Portland enjoys a more diversified leisure time sports scene than most other Maine communities. Entertainment and recreation are a part of daily life here, and I have devoted a section to these activities, though they are apart from the phoenix theme.

Many of the photographs contained within have never been published. I am grateful for being given the opportunity to use the archives of the Jewish Community Center; these archives are still in the process of being catalogued, and I was the first person allowed to use the virgin material as a resource. This material has contributed significantly to the book.

As with the other books I've done, this work on Portland is dedicated to the city's younger people. I hope that the many photographs will compete successfully with television for their interest. Local history is a subject that is all too often overlooked by our system of education; it is hoped that this book and the others in the series will give the younger people a sense of their community's history, and by doing so, fill in that gap in their education.

One

The Phoenix Factor

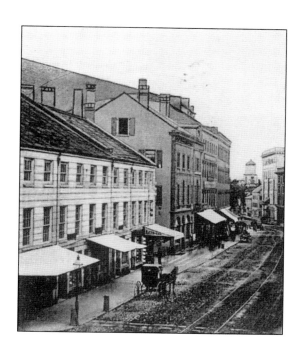

Middle Street, one of Portland's busiest streets, is shown here in a view from Union Street. The date is 1863, three years before the great Portland fire.

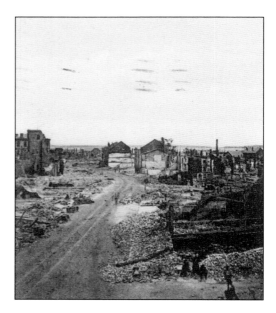

This photograph, looking down Middle Street from Free Street, was taken after the Great Fire of July 4, 1866. The fire made more than 10,000 homeless, and over 1,500 homes and business places were leveled.

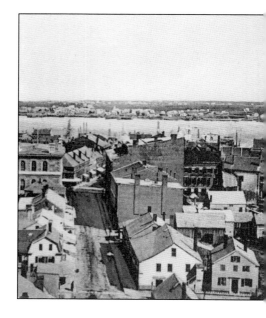

Exchange Street, another of Portland's busiest streets, is shown here in 1863 in a view from the dome of Portland City Hall.

Here we are looking up Exchange Street from Fore Street after the Fire of 1866.

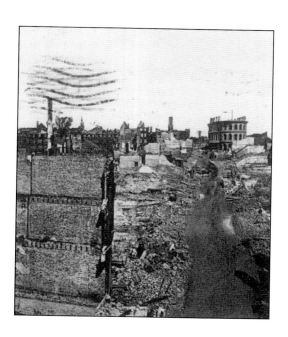

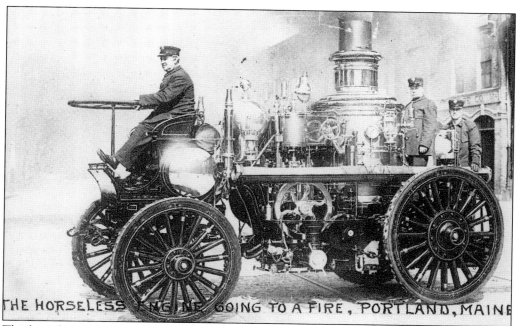

THE HORSELESS ENGINE GOING TO A FIRE, PORTLAND, MAINE

This horseless engine is going to a fire in Portland in the early 1900s. There were no such engines in 1866. In addition, there was a water shortage to fight the great Portland fire; reservoirs were soon emptied and the nearby ocean was at low tide.

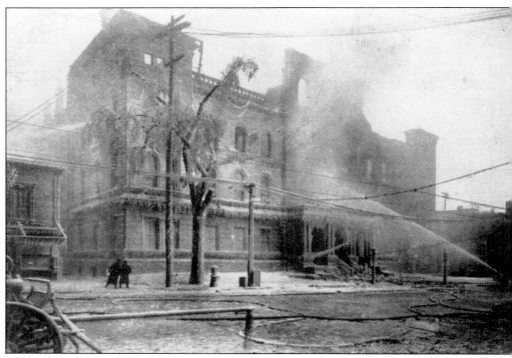

The ruins of Portland City Hall are shown here on the morning of January 24, 1908.

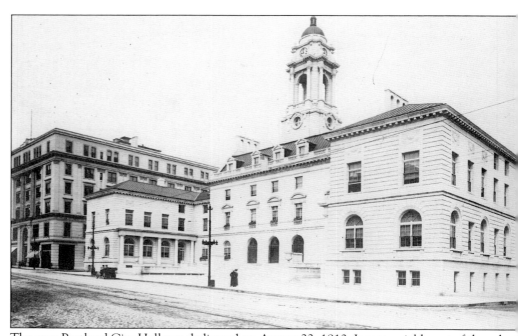

The new Portland City Hall was dedicated on August 22, 1912. It rose quickly out of the ashes.
The Masonic Building stands next to it.

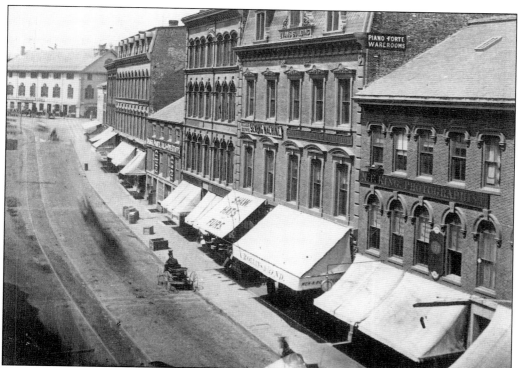

Middle Street, looking toward the old city hall, is shown here in the 1870s. Compare this with the picture of Middle Street just after the Fire of 1866. Good things can rise from ashes.

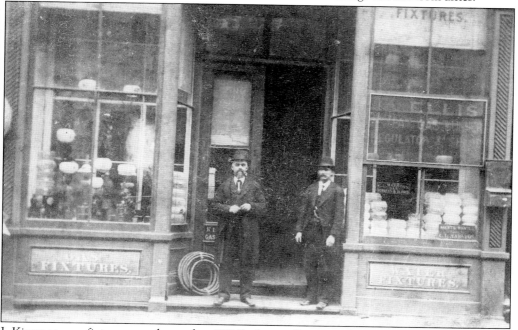

J. Kinsman, gas fixtures, was located at 128 Exchange Street in the 1870s. Again, consider the earlier picture of Exchange Street just after the Fire of 1866.

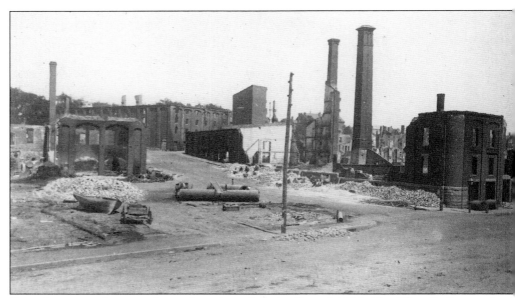

Brown's sugar refinery is shown here just after the Fire of 1866. The West Indian trade, in which lumber was exported in return for molasses and raw sugar, formed the basis of J.I Brown's fortune.

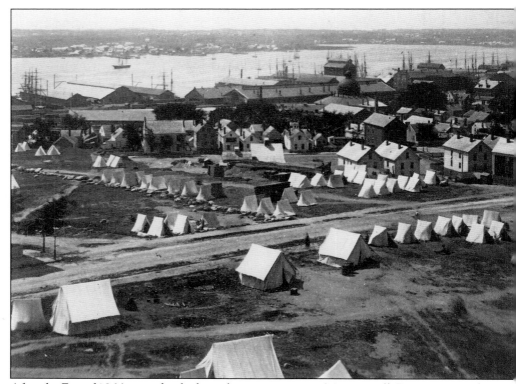

After the Fire of 1866, tents for the homeless were set up on Munjoy Hill. For a time, similar tent appeared in other burned-out sections of the city. This view is from the Portland Observatory.

Two

Phoenix Expanded

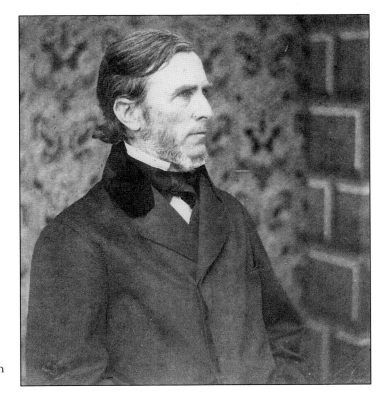

William Pitt Fessenden is an example of the high-minded politicians who sometimes came from the ranks of the relatively wealthy, old-line families who ruled the political roost in Portland before the turn of the century. As a U.S. Senator, he voted against the impeachment of President Andrew Johnson, and he was not reelected as a result. He held several high-ranking cabinet posts in Washington, and is shown here in the late 1860s.

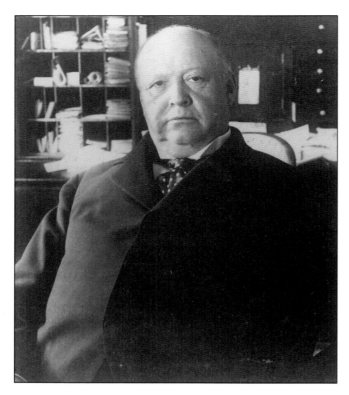

Even more imposing on the national political scene was Thomas Brackett Reed of Portland, shown here about 1898. As speaker of the U.S. House of Representatives, Reed ran the operation with a tight enough hand so he was called "Czar" Reed.

Reed even had a cigar named after him. Cook, Everett, and Pennell was a Portland drug and sundry firm. One wonders how this cigar went in the smoke-filled rooms where political deal were made.

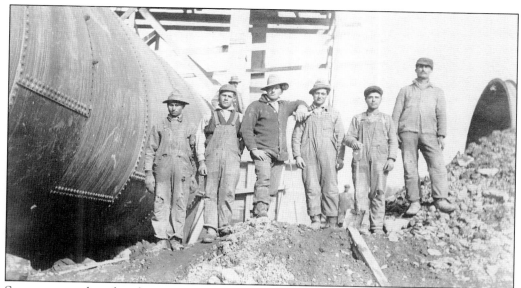

Soon a new political and social force was at hand, rising from the ashes of the countries from which it had come to Portland. The Irish often worked on the Portland waterfront. So did the Italians. Vincenzo Reali is one of those above.

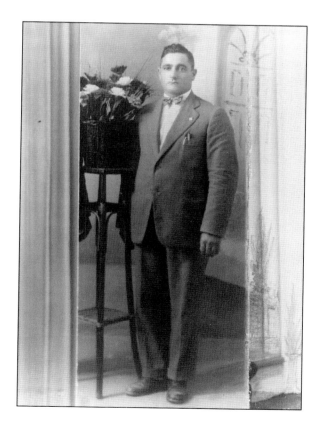

Vincenzo Reali is shown here in his late twenties or early thirties. Reali was the founder of the Village Cafe, now one of Portland's most famous restaurants.

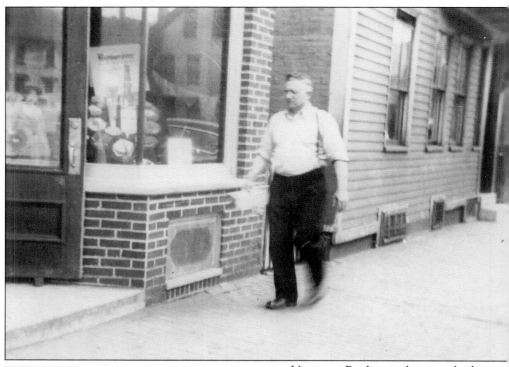

Vincenzo Reali was photographed in the 1930s by the original Village Cafe. The restaurant, on Newbury Street, was later enlarged.

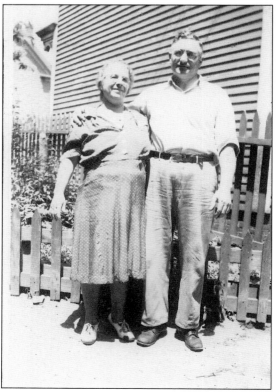

Vincenzo and Maria Aceto Reali are shown here in their later years. Vincenzo came to Portland from Ciprano, about 9 miles south of Rome. His wife came from Monatella, near Pescara in Italy.

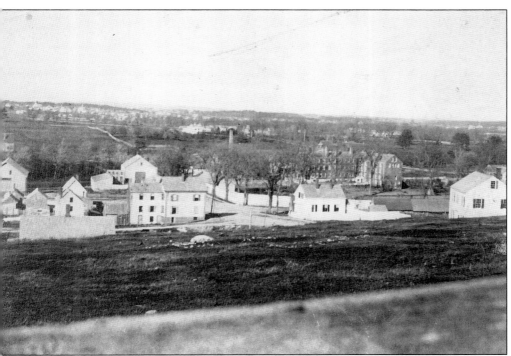

There were income discrepancies in Portland before the turn of the century, as this 1870s photograph shows. Some rose out of the ashes of poverty; some didn't.

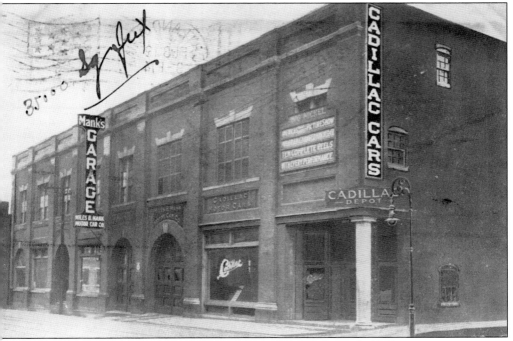

Mank's Garage in Portland sold Cadillacs to the wealthy in the early 1910s.

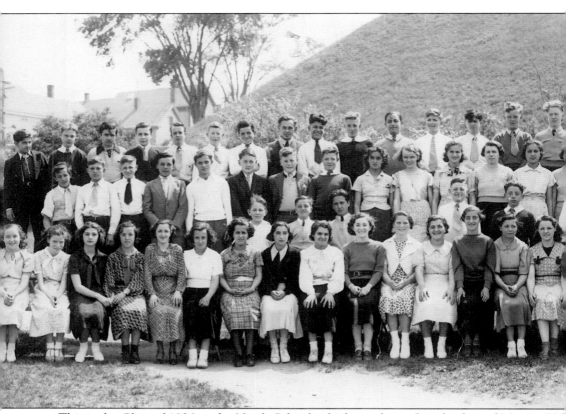

This is the Class of 1936 at the North School, which was located at the foot of Munjoy Hill on Congress Street. Many children from low-income families or families of immigrants attended this school. Among those in the first row are Nora McDonough, Connie Oppedisano, a Salamone, Jennie Aceto, two Ciampis, one Monderelle, Arlene Lynch, Mary Nappi, Virginia Ricchio, Mary DeDominicus, Louise Cavallero, Paul McIntyre, Mildred Russo, Mary Fantasia, Mrs. Frank Lapurmada, Grace Citucci (Morano), Rose Cirillo, one Bellino, Lena DiPaulo, another Salamone, Mickalino Fasulo, and one Mancini. Some of those in the second row are Gerald Dwight, Sammy Tucci, Henry Bardi, Joseph Primo, Keith Brogan, one Germaine

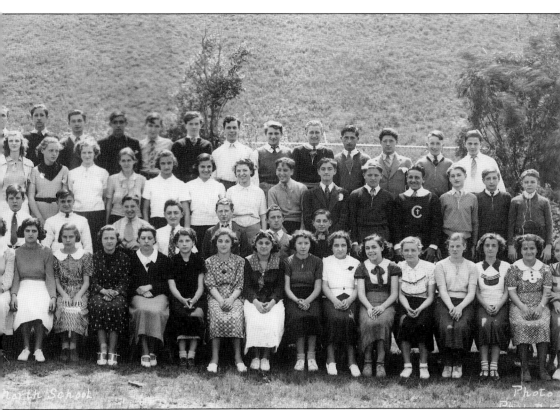

Johnny Isdorian, Santino Cardilli, Rudolph Ferrante, one Jordan, Tomasina Lancia, Alice Hinds, John DiBiase, and Al Reali. In the third row, among others, we have Genero Dadiego, Harold Punsky, Orlando Sisti, Frank Fasulo, Frank Conant, Amedeo Palanzo, one Catrano, Antoinette D'Alfonso, Ann Driscoll, Sally Cinder (D'Alfonso), one DiMatteo, Tony Albino, Lawrence Corridini, William Orr, and Joe D'Alfonso. Finally, in the fourth row, there are Paul Vinella, Joe Buck, Richard Manoogian, Francis Cavallaro, Alvin Holt, Philip Paglio, Minnie Lynch, Tony Ricci, one Bethune, Frederick Harris, one Calvert, one Guptill, one Lancia, Frank Polotzi, Lewis Waxman, Louis Botto, Taviano Breggia, Peter Bellino, and Joseph Bove.

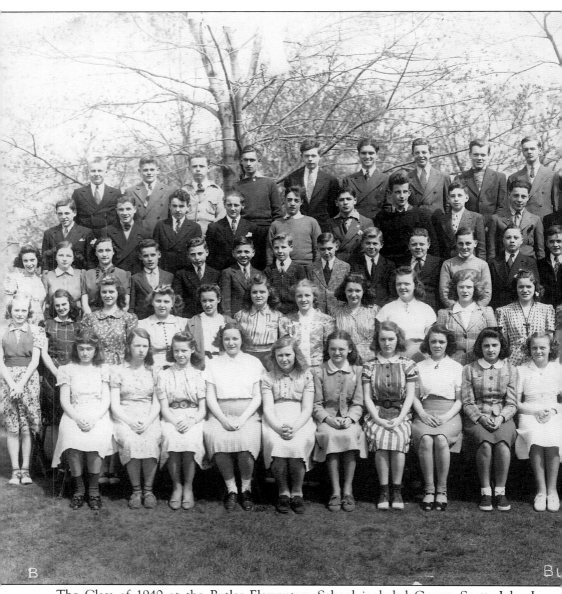

The Class of 1940 at the Butler Elementary School included George Scott, John Lyons, Paul Zdanowicz, Robert Rosen, Archie Lomac, Ray Troubh, Frank Ahern, Clyde F. Dinsmore, Carl Raymond, Eugene Parker, Calvin Shur, Ralph Conant, Leonard Larain, John Harrigan, Morton Slosberg, Sherman Gilson, Robert Lowell, Robert Komar, Charles Hastings, Arthur Upham, Stephen Fifield, George Gormley, Kenneth Stokes, Lester L. Buck, John Furnas, Earl Fenderson, Richard Wilson, Gordon Beam, Parker Poole Jr., Mildred E. Little,

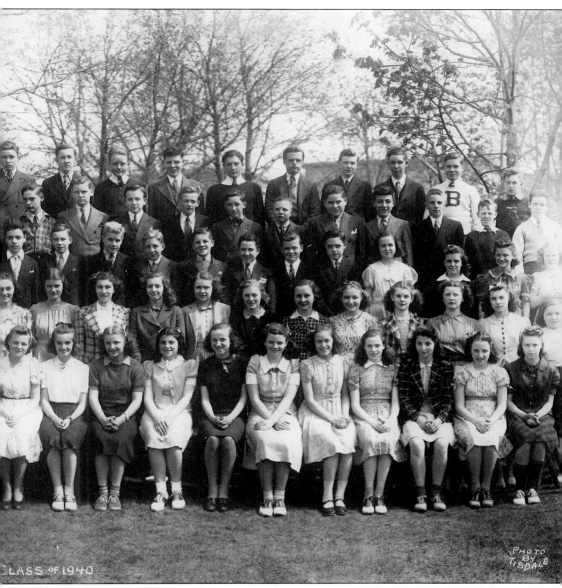

CLASS OF 1940

L. Pauline Mann, Jimmie Blanchard, Roland Holmes, Marcia L. Blumenthal, Jean Hight, Barbara Thompson, Phyllis Crowell, Evelyn Shur, Hope Fenderson, Marjoria Kennedy, Harriett Cary, R.W. Lyons, Shirley Scanlin, Phyllis Jones, Ruth E. Teed, Barbara L. Needelman, A. Everett Strout, Carl Leboire, Josephine Fagone, Marjoria Bernard, Helen Danilewicz, and Warren Reeves.

23

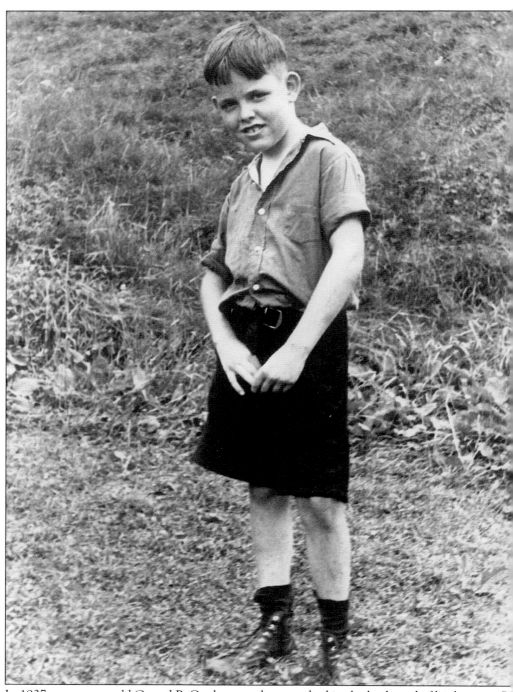

In 1937, seven-year-old Gerard P. Conley was photographed in the back yard of his home at 7 Payson Street. Portland elected Republicans as its state legislators for many years, until Edmund S. Muskie was elected governor as a Democrat in 1954. Within a few years, Portland's legislative delegation became almost solidly Democratic. Conley rose to become president of the Maine State Senate from 1983 to 1985.

Conley, now thirteen years old, was photographed in 1943 at the Sacred Heart Grammar School.

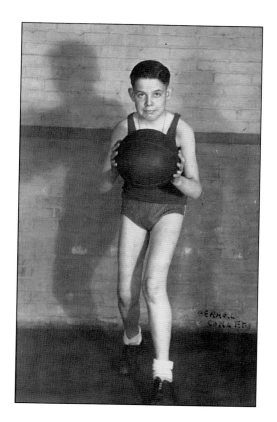

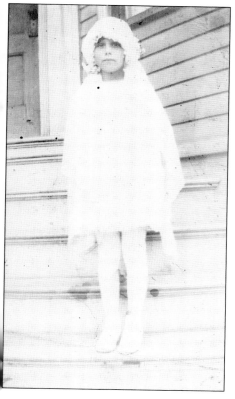

Catherine Forbes (Carswell) is shown here at her 36 Fox Street home the day of her first Holy Communion in the late 1920s. She was to become a state representative and a state senator during the Democratic rising in Portland.

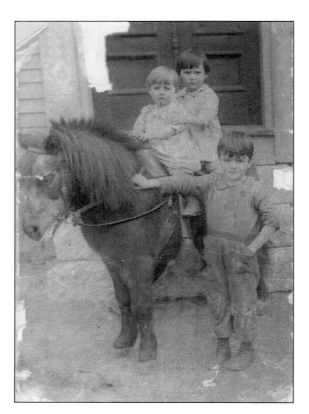

Catherine and John Forbes are on and beside a pony in the late 1920s. John was severely wounded in World War II. The child in the front is Magaret Forbes Reali.

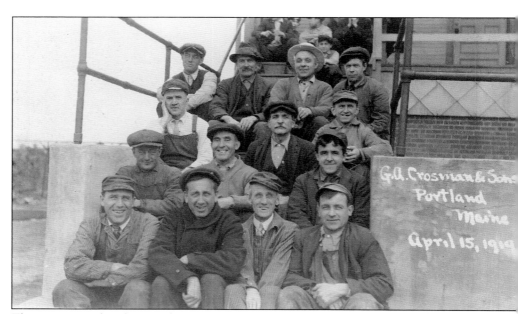

This is a group of workers on the steps of the J.A. Crosman & Sons building in Portland on April 15, 1919. They were some of the "little people" who became the backbone of the Democratic uprising in Portland in the mid-1950s.

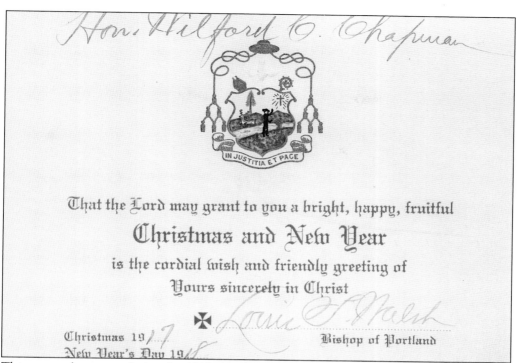

Hon. Wilford C. Chapman

That the Lord may grant to you a bright, happy, fruitful

Christmas and New Year

is the cordial wish and friendly greeting of

Yours sincerely in Christ

✠ _Louis S. Walsh_

Christmas 19/7
New Year's Day 19/8

Bishop of Portland

This postcard was sent during the 1917–18 Christmas season from the Most Rev. Louis Walsh, bishop of the Roman Catholic Diocese of Portland (covering all of Maine), to the Honorable Wilford C. Chapman. Many of the immigrants coming to Portland were Roman Catholics. The Church was active in giving aid to them when needed and in helping them to begin anew in Portland.

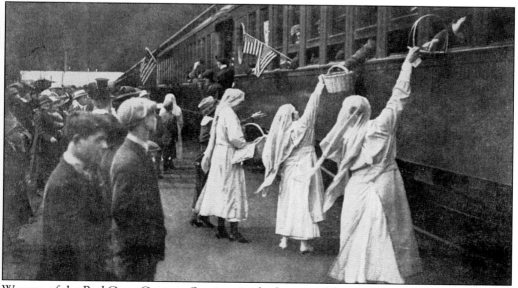

Women of the Red Cross Canteen Service give baskets to soldiers at Union Station in October 1918. Both World War I and World War II increased the social mobility of many living in Portland.

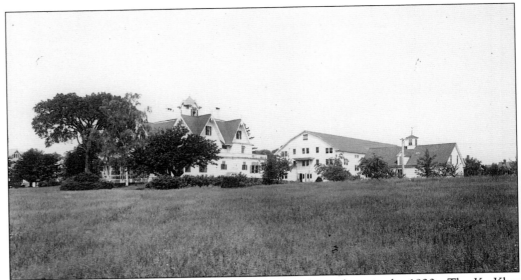

The Witham Klavern and Klub House in Portland is shown here in the 1920s. The Ku Klux Klan became very active and quite popular in Portland from 1921 to 1924. Eugene "Doc" Farnsworth, a Columbia Falls native, was the King Kleagle of the Klan in Maine's largest city. With few blacks in Maine, the KKK was especially active in this state against Catholics. The KKK headquarters was on Forest Avenue. Farnsworth, who was eventually expelled by the KKK, set up a somewhat similar group on his own. He died in 1926.

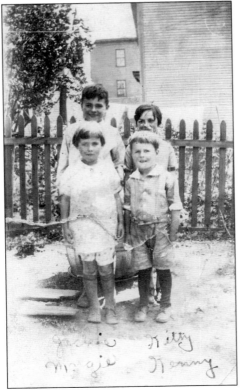

Margaret and Kenneth Forbes (front) and John and Kitty (Catherine) Forbes (rear) were photographed together in the late 1920s. Their father, John, worked as a house painter, and then owned his own grocery store and fish market at the corner of Cumberland Avenue and Franklin Street. Mrs. Forbes worked at Burnham and Morrill and Greeley Laundry. John became ill and died of cancer in 1941.

Hubert Reali, one of Vincenzo Reali's sons, is shown here at his confirmation in 1937.

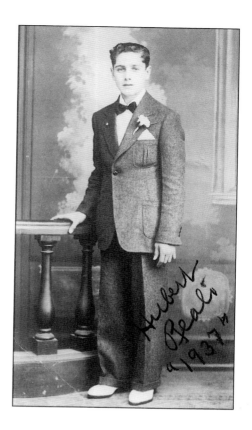

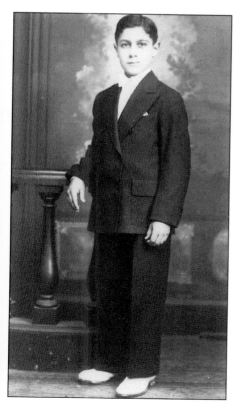

Amadeo Reali, another son of Vincenzo, was photographed in his confirmation suit in the late 1930s.

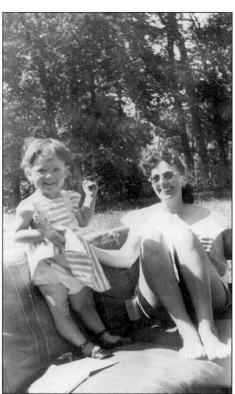

Catherine Forbes (right) and Sandra Reali (Whitten) posed in 1944 at 84 Parsons Road.

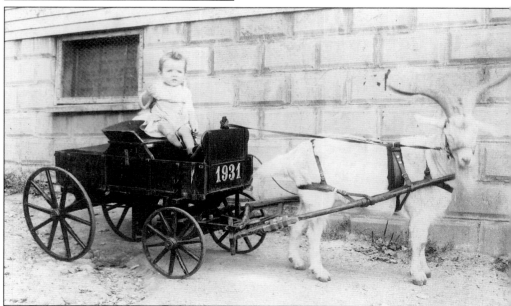

William Forbes was very young when he was photographed in the early 1930s in a goat cart. At the age of thirteen, Bill Forbes saved the life of nine-year-old Angelo Liponis, after a raft that Liponis was riding capsized near Tukey's Bridge. This was in August 1944. Forbes jumped in the water and made a courageous rescue.

Simon Moulton Hamlin was elected the U.S. Representative from Maine's First Congressional District in 1934. He served one term from 1935 to 1937. A Democrat, Hamlin was part of a small Democratic breakthrough in the state caused by the depression. "Will stay with the forgotten man for I am one," was part of his campaign platform. Portland was included in the district.

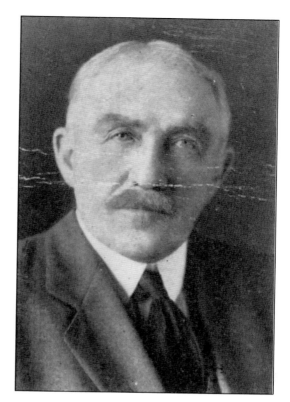

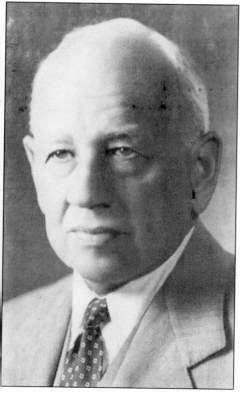

Robert Hale was the first district congressman from 1943 to 1959. Hale, a Republican, came from Portland and had the right last name. Eugene Hale was the U.S. Senator from Maine from 1881 to 1911, while Frederick Hale held the same post from 1917 to 1941. Robert Hale was eventually beaten by Republican-turned-Democrat James C. Oliver, as the Maine Democrats built their strength.

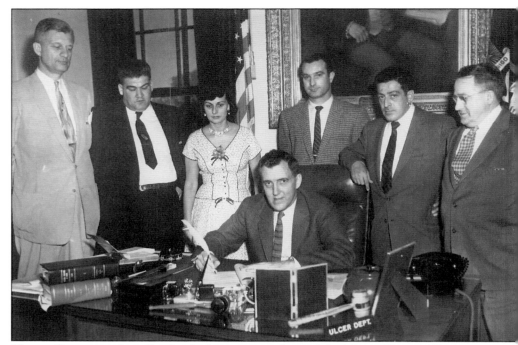

The six Democrats from Portland who were members of the Maine House of Representative got together in 1957 after the big Democratic win. The seventh member of the Portland House delegation was Dana W. Childs, a Republican who later became a Democrat. From left to right with Governor Edmund S. Muskie in the front, are Thomas Maynard, Edward (Bing) Miller Catherine Forbes Carswell, Richard Broderick, Caspar Tevanian, and Alfred Smith.

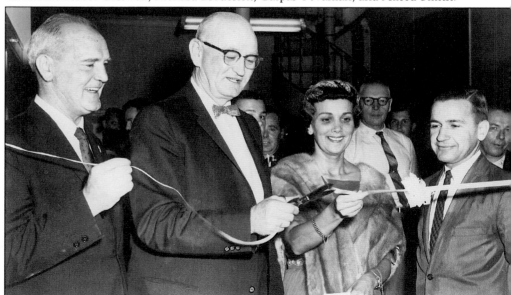

Opening Democratic headquarters in Portland in 1959 were Ted Brownlee (state representative and city chairman), James C. Oliver (who won the congressional seat), State Representative Catherine Hendricks Carswell, and Clyde Bartlett (who was working for Oliver).

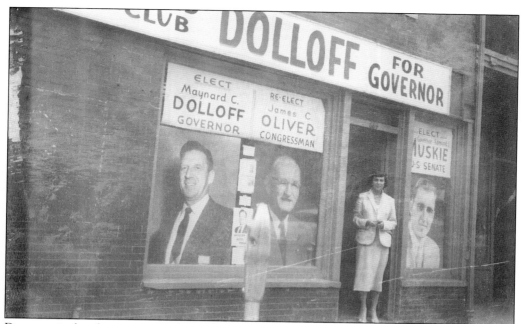

Democratic headquarters was located at 664A Congress Street in Portland on June 16, 1958. State Representative Catherine Carswell stands in front of pictures of the Democratic candidates: Maynard Dolloff for governor; James C. Oliver for first district congressman; and Governor Edmund S. Muskie for the U.S. Senate.

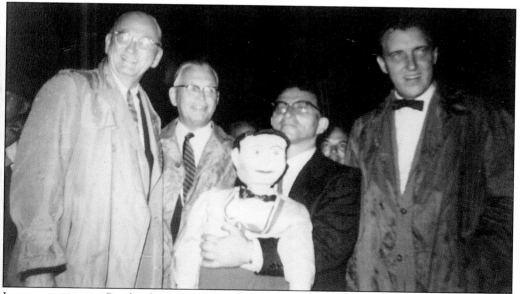

It was pouring in Portland's Monument Square on September 7, 1958, the Sunday before Election Day (it was still in September). From left to right are: James C. Oliver, who was elected first district congressman; Clinton Clauson, elected governor; David Glovsky with his dummy (Dave is best known for guessing people's weights at Old Orchard Beach); and Governor Edmund S. Muskie, who was elected to the U.S. Senate. It was one of the peaks of Democratic power in Portland and Maine.

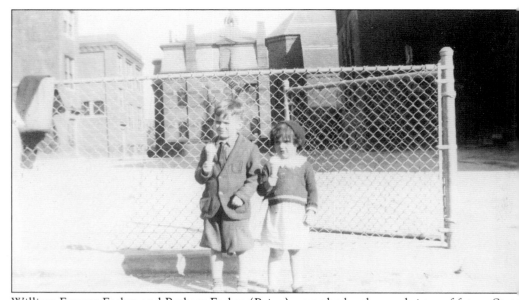

William Everett Forbes and Barbara Forbes (Paine) were the brother and sister of future State Representative and State Senator Catherine Forbes Carswell. They are shown here at the St. Aloysius (Cathedral) Grammar School on May 18, 1937, during the depths of the depression.

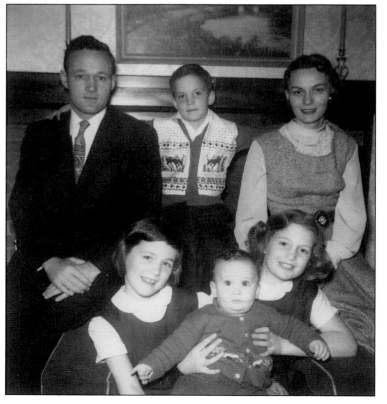

The Dana W. Childs family posed for a photograph in 1956. Childs was still a Republican at this time, and was the majority leader in the Maine House of Representatives. Later, Dana became a Democrat and was Speaker of the House. From left to right are: (front row) Michele, Billy, and Donna; (back row) Dana, Dana, and Jean. The political balance in Portland had shifted and hasn't yet turned around. Most of the Democratic stalwarts had risen from the ashes of the depression.

Three

The Jewish Community

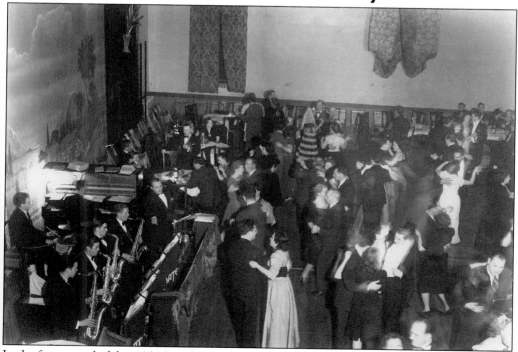

In the foreground of this 1939 Jewish Community Center dance are Irving and Anne Rothstein, Philip Reuben and Fefe Stern, and Harold and Millie Nelson. There were few Jewish people in Portland until the 1880s, because most originally located in the larger cities of this country. When Jewish people immigrated here, they came primarily from the Eastern European countries that were part of the Russian Empire.

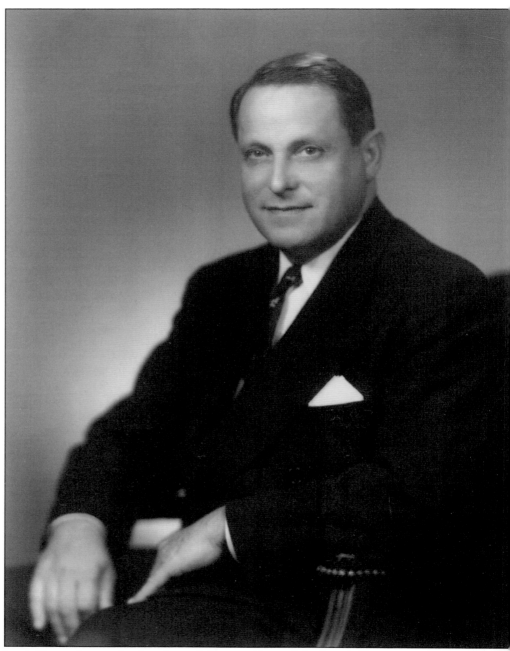

Louis Bernstein was the founder and first president of the Jewish Community Center. A 192.
Bowdoin College graduate, Bernstein raised more money for that college than any previou
individual. An Air Force major in World War II, he was later a Portland Municipal Cour
judge. The Jewish community paid $17,500 in 1937 for the former Knights of Pythias Buildin,
on Cumberland Avenue. It served as the JCC building for almost fifty years.

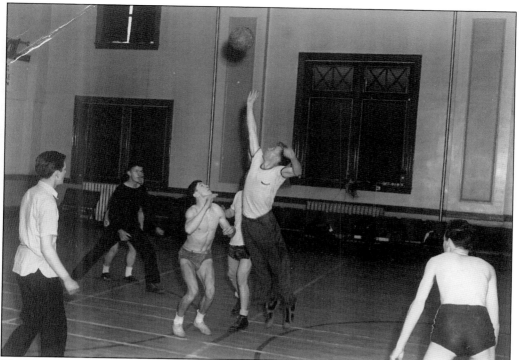

The JCC served as a center for all activities of the Jewish community and, thus, served as a focus point for the several synagogues in Portland. In addition, the JCC allowed its building to be used by other organizations.

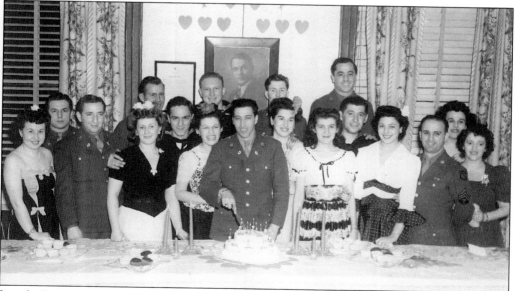

Jewish Community Center women are shown here entertaining for the USO during World War II. Among them are Harriet Kroot Weisman, Gladys Potter, Mildred Brenner Schwartz, Ruth Karlin Finn, Dorothy Cohen, Ina Schatz Weissman, Annabelle Boxstein Mack, and Rae Modes Wolf.

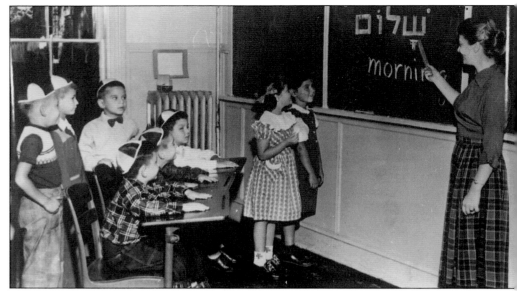

This photograph of a Hebrew lesson dates from the 1940s.

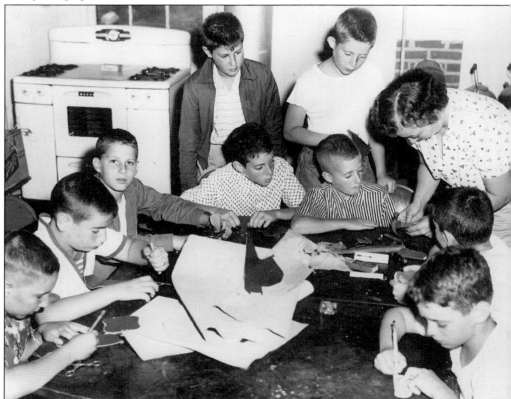

A JCC youth group receives instruction from Mrs. Radcliffe in the 1940s. From left to right are: (front row) Donald Warner, Donnie Levi, Mark Willis, Harris Gleckman, Joel Karlick, Gary Taylor, and Duane Polisner; (back row) Steve Slotsky and John Campton.

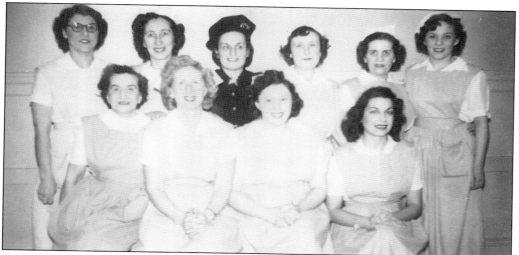

A senior Hadassah choral group was photographed at the Jewish Community Center in the 1940s or '50s. From left to right are: (front row) Mrs. David Perlin, Mrs. Harry Goldberg, Mrs. Max Millstein, and Mrs. Joseph Kornhauser; (back row) Mrs. William Stewart, Mrs. Herman Gershenson, Mrs. Louis Shatz (music chairman), Mrs. Maurice Levine, Mrs. Sam Kates, and Mrs. Sidney Levine (co-chairperson).

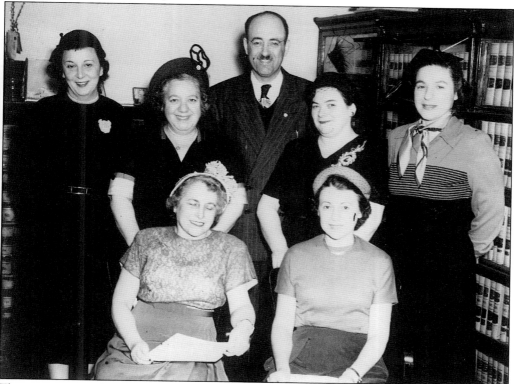

This group was at the JCC in the 1950s. From left to right are: (front row) Mrs. William Punsky and Mrs. Robert Mack; (back row) Mrs. Maurice Sandler, Mrs. Benjamin Lerman, Irving Rothstein (co-chairperson), Mrs. Morris Richman, and Mrs. Sidney Wernick.

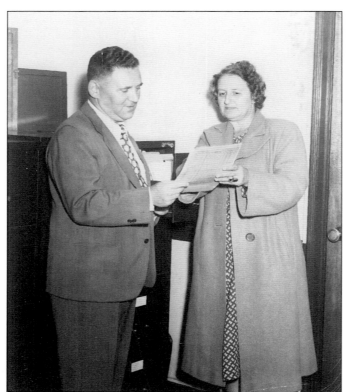

Barnett I. Shur, a former JCC president and corporation counsel for the City of Portland for many years, talks the figures over with an unknown individual in the 1940s. Shur was a Maine leader in municipal law.

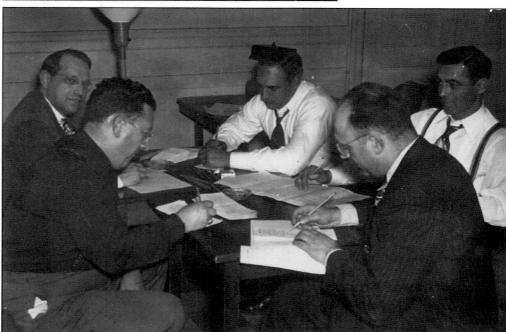

Arnold Goodman, Maurice Davis, James Ross, Bud Kane, and Irving Rothstein were deep in JCC business when this photograph was taken in the 1950s.

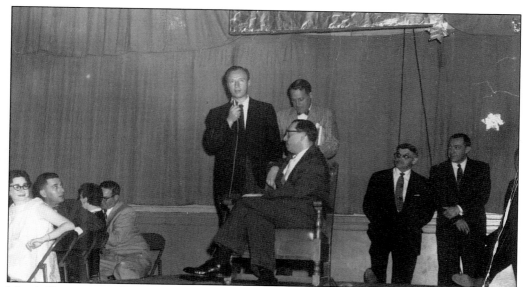

Morris Cox was installed as the JCC president in 1954. Harold P. Nelson is at the microphone with Judge Louis Bernstein behind him. On the right are Edward Berman and Harold Potter.

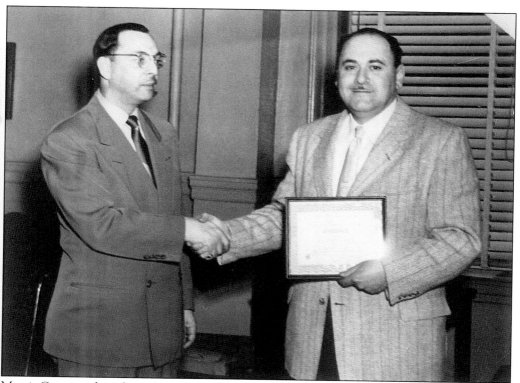

Morris Cox was also a long-time clerk of the U.S. District Court in Portland. He is shown here with a certificate of appreciation for then Democratic State Representative Arnold Briggs.

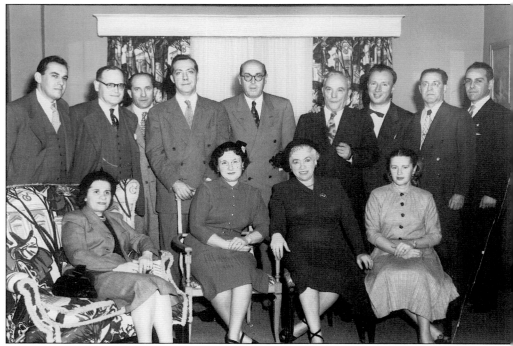

These are some of the powers-that-were at the JCC in the 1950s. From left to right are (seated) Mrs. Samuel Kates, Mrs. Maurice Levine, and Mrs. Harold Nelson; (standing) Louis J Michaelson, Israel Bernstein, Benjamin Lewis, Harold J. Potter, Philip W. Lown, Abraham S Levey, Harold Nelson, Benjamin Lazarus, and Benjamin Hagai.

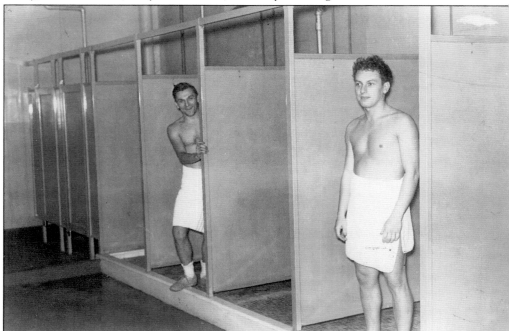

Phil Schilling and Sidney Miller were photographed in the JCC's mens showers in 1938.

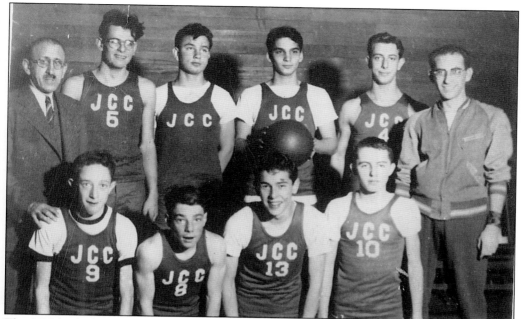

This JCC basketball team, probably from the 1940s, consisted of: (front row) Stan Fink, Murray Reuben, Alvan Mersky, and Billy Matson; (back row) Ben Troen, Harry Offenberg, Chuck Mack, Ken Waks, Irv Zalcman, and Coach Dean Silverman. There are now several thousand members of Portland's Jewish community. They have provided service to their city, state, and country far beyond their numbers.

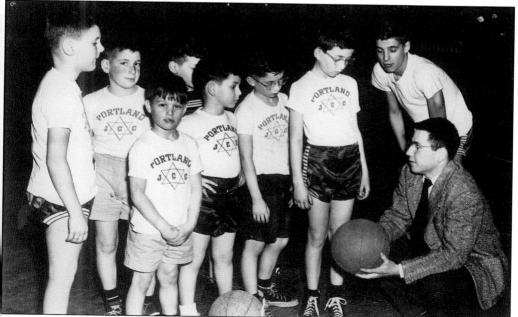

More JCC basketball, this time in the 1950s. From left to right are George Shur, Jeffrey Weinstein, Marty Brenerman, Jim Baker, Elliott Lerman, Bob Rodman, Larry Cohen, and Ernie Loeb.

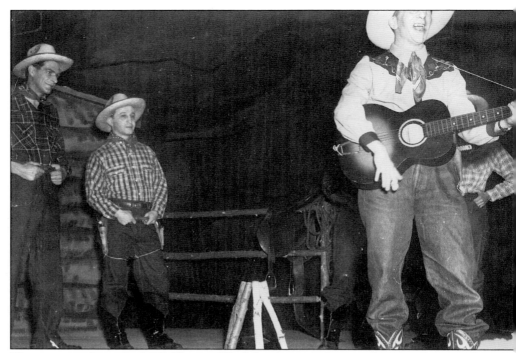

This scene is from the JCC Theater Workshop's original musical revue, *Front And Center.*
It featured Frank Laben, Yudy Elowitch, and Edward Victor, and ran in the 1940s or '50.
Theatrical productions were a very important part of the JCC program. Many excellent actor,
actresses, and production people were turned out.

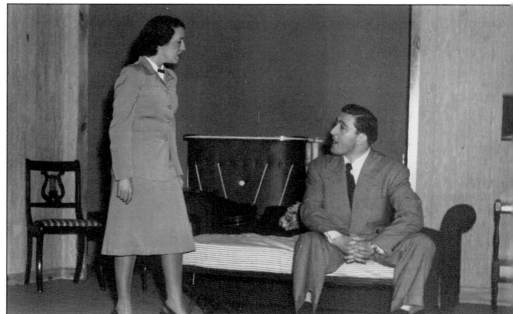

Beatrice Waxman and Arnold Potter emote at a JCC Theater Workshop production i
the 1950s.

The JCC Theater Workshop *Claudia* featured, from left to right, Mrs. Yoland Potter, Frances Levine, and Mrs. Icky Abramson in the 1940s.

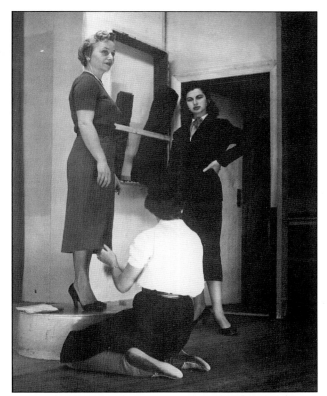

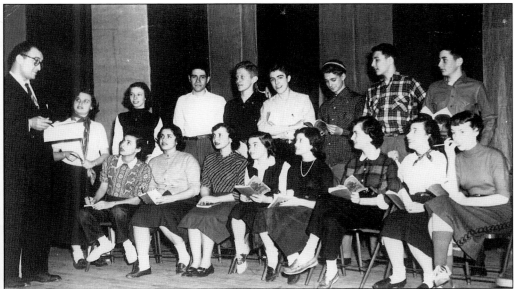

Hal Schneiderman directs a group for the JCC production of *Growing Pains* in the 1950s. From left to right are: (front row) Merle Royte (Nelson), Mona Loeb, Joanne Silverman, Rhona Merdek, Linda Lavin (who went on to stage and TV fame), Diann Garon, Verna Posner, and unknown; (back row) Barbara Nevins, Lonette Renlik, Neil Lucke, Donald Cutler, Norman Finberg, Larry Kane, Mike Ross, and David Weisberg.

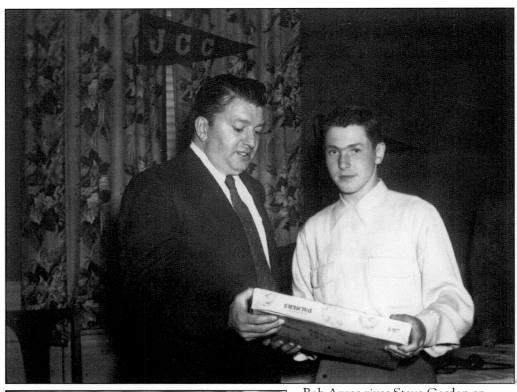

Bob Agger gives Steve Gordon an award at the 1953 JCC Sports Night.

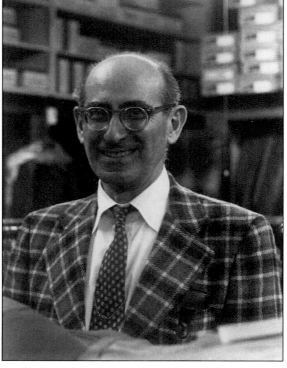

Israel (Dean) Silverman was a leader in the JCC's sports activities and the coach of many JCC teams.

Mrs. Joseph Taylor won the funniest prize at a JCC function in the 1950s.

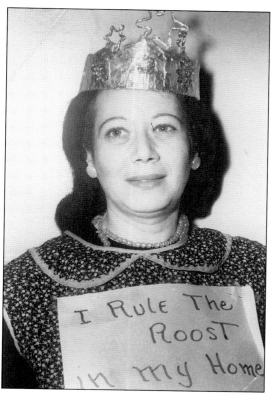

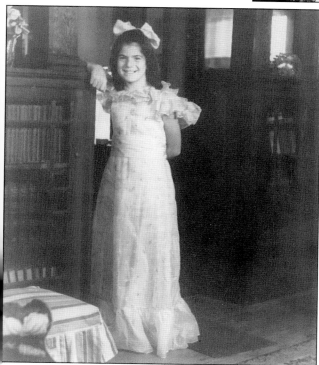

Evelyn Green Litman is shown here in 1939 at the age of eight.

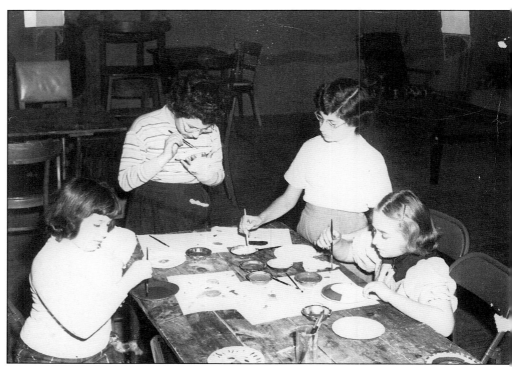

The JCC vacation jamboree in 1947 featured arts, crafts, and, from left to right, Beverly Potte. Linda Elowitch Abromson, unknown, and Sandy Karlick.

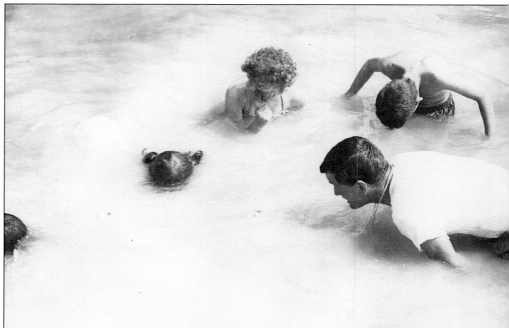

The JCC Day Camp was located at Sebago Lake in 1948 or 1949. Bert Baucher, a waterfron instructor and lifeguard, instructs his youngsters "to dip their heads in the water."

It's pie eating time at a JCC picnic in the 1950s. JCC Executive Director Victor Taylor is officiating.

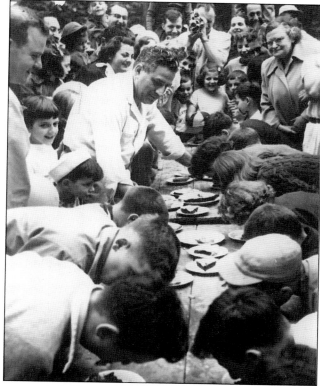

At the JCC Day Camp in 1954 were Janice Newman, Elinor Pachowsky, Barbara Young, Roberta Citrin, Paula Rosengard, Susie Greenman, Cynthia Rudolf, Clair Lerman, Claire Appel, and Deb Loeb.

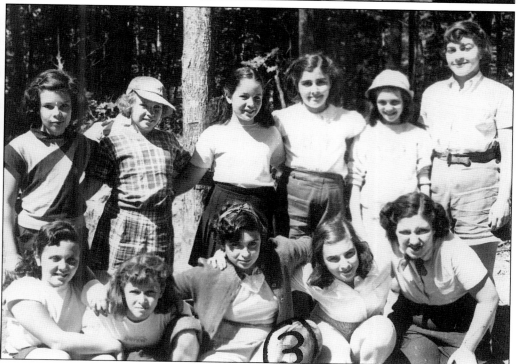

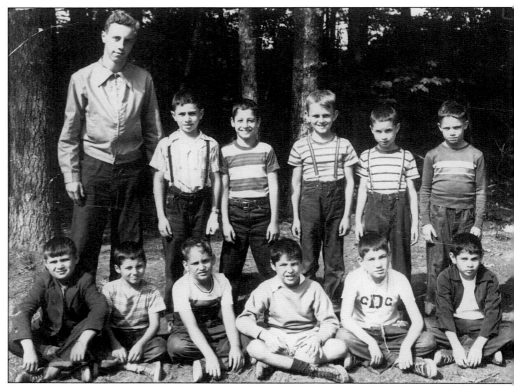

Some of those in this 1940s photograph of the JCC Day Camp are Eddie Webber, Stevi Joachim, Stevie Willis, Stewart Potter, Mel Zimelman, Kenny Davidson, Stanley Elowitch Donald Cutler, Lennie Slosberg, and Joe Gordon.

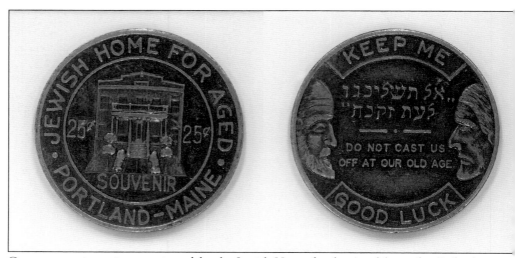

Commemorative coins were issued for the Jewish Home for the Aged (now the Cedars).

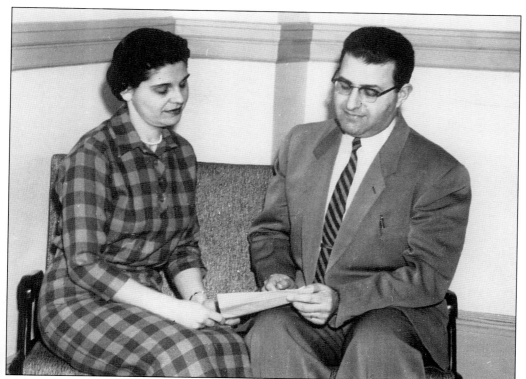

Melvin Stone, who owned several radio stations, and his wife Frances discuss a JCC program at the center in the 1950s.

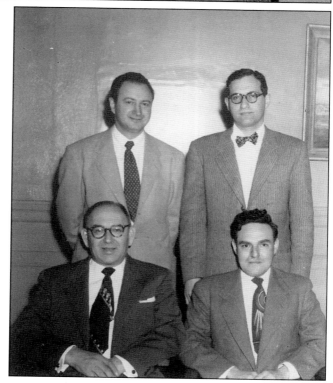

This 1950s photograph of some strong JCC workers shows, from left to right: (seated) unknown and Harold E. Ross; (standing) Dr. Henry Pollard and Sumner T. Bernstein.

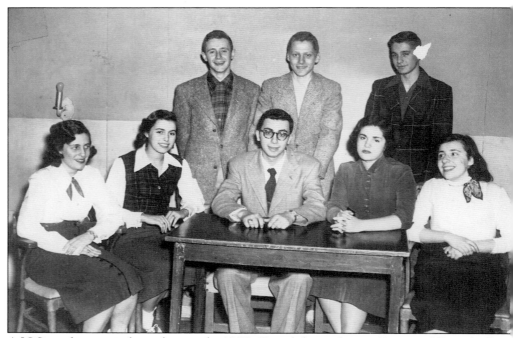

A JCC youth group is shown here in the 1950s. From left to right are: (front row) Dorothy Bres Merle Royte (Nelson), Jerry Sandler, Malka Loew, and Adele Glovsky; (back row) Leonar Nelson, Donny Cutler, and Larry Kane.

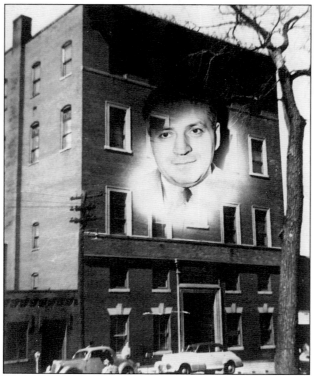

This is the former JCC building, with long-time Executive Directo Victor Taylor superimposed.

Four

Doers and Shakers

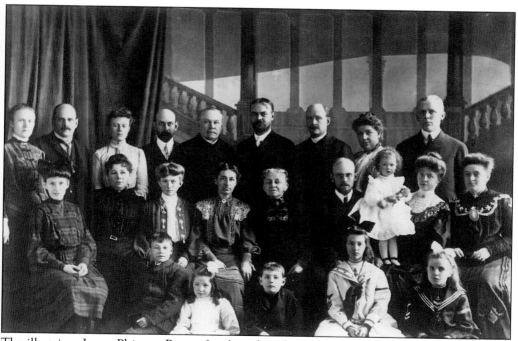

The illustrious James Phinney Baxter family gathered together for Thanksgiving in 1904. From left to right are: (front row) James P. Baxter III, Emily W. Baxter, John L. Baxter, Ellen L. Baxter, and Emily M. Baxter; (middle row) Sarah B. Baxter, Mrs. Eugene R. Baxter, Cara D. Baxter, Mrs. Hartley C. Baxter, Mrs. James P. Baxter Sr., Rupert H. Baxter, Mary Baxter, Mrs. Rupert H. Baxter, and Mrs. Clinton D. Baxter; (back row) Emily P. Baxter, Clinton L. Baxter, Madeline C. Baxter, Eugene R. Baxter, James Phinney Baxter Sr. (the six-time Portland mayor), James P. Baxter Jr., Hartley C. Baxter, Mrs. James P. Baxter Jr., and future Maine Governor Percival P. Baxter. James P. Baxter Sr. had eight children by two wives.

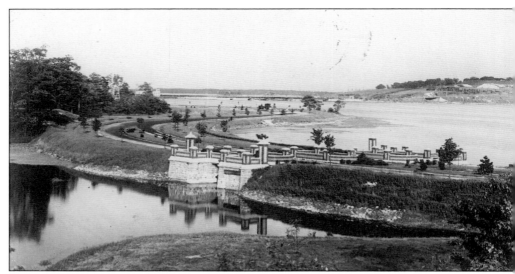

Baxter Boulevard is shown here in the early 1930s. It was given the city by James Phinney Baxter Sr., who also had Frederick Olmsted work out a park plan for Portland.

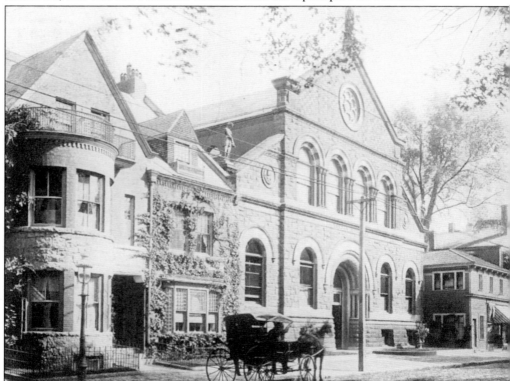

The Portland Public Library was located on Congress Street in the early 1900s. It was donated to the city by six-time Portland Mayor James Phinney Baxter Sr. It was closed in 1979 when a new library was built, and is now part of the Portland College of Art. Baxter's son, Governor Percival P. Baxter, eclipsed his father by giving Baxter State Park (including Mount Katahdin) to the state, as well as the Baxter School for the Deaf on Mackworth Island.

This photograph, taken in August 1942, shows three generations of the Thomas family, which included three presidents of the Canal National Bank at Brentwood (the Thomas home). The bank was controlled by the Thomas family from 1849 to 1979, and the bank's headquarters were located in Portland. Sixty-nine-year-old William Widgery Thomas II was also president of the Maine Savings Bank in Portland, holding both bank presidencies at the same time. To the left is forty-one-year-old Widgery Thomas, another Canal president. To the right is eighteen-year-old Widgery Thomas Jr., a student at Bowdoin College. The Canal National Bank existed from 1826 to 1982, when it merged into Depositors Trust Company.

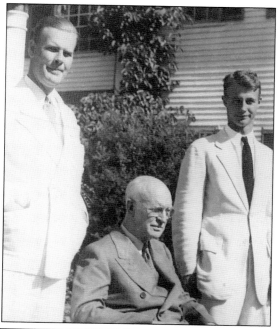

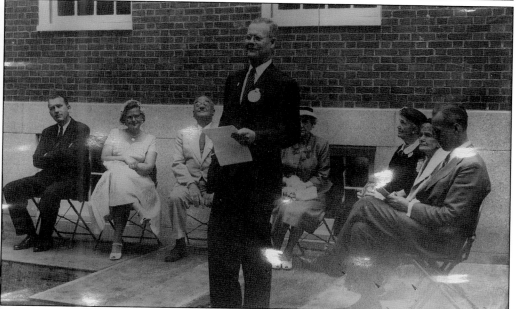

Widgery Thomas, then president of the Canal National Bank, speaks at the dedication of Coleman Hall at Bowdoin College. The Portland-Bowdoin connection has always been strong, especially with the Bowdoin Class of 1922, to which Thomas belonged. Thomas was chairman of the building committee for both Coleman Hall and Bowdoin's Senior Center. To the right is Bowdoin President James S. Coles. Several members of the Coleman family were present, as was John Pickard, also a member of the Class of 1922. Pickard, shown here looking up at Thomas's right, was a retired Dupont executive who gave great amounts of money and the Pickard Theater to the college.

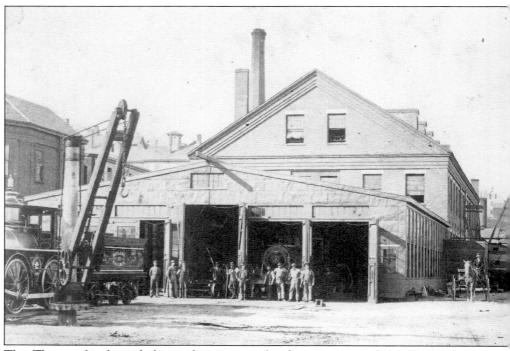

The Thomas family and their relatives owned a large portion of the Portland Company locomotive works in the 1870s. They made their money from banking, and were directly descended from the first settlers of Portland. The Baxters, another powerful Portland family, made their fortune in the canning industry, and could trace their roots back to the start of American history. The two families, as pillars of Portland, helped greatly when the city needed to rise from the ashes.

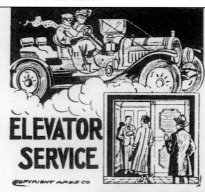

DOES YOUR ELEVATOR BELONG TO A BYGONE DAY?

Or is it a truly modern convey-ance with attractive car, devices which make it move smoothly, swiftly and accurately.

If your elevator is not giving this service, we will be glad to ex-plain to you how it can be modern-ized at low cost. Repairing, remod-elling and maintenance of all types of elevators—is our specialty.

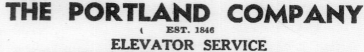

THE PORTLAND COMPANY
(EST. 1846
ELEVATOR SERVICE
MANUFACTURERS OF ELEVATORS
Repairing - Inspection - Modernizing

A Portland Company ad for elevators in the 1910s asks: "Does Your Elevator Belong To A Bygone Day?" The company was established in 1846 and operated into the second half of the twentieth century.

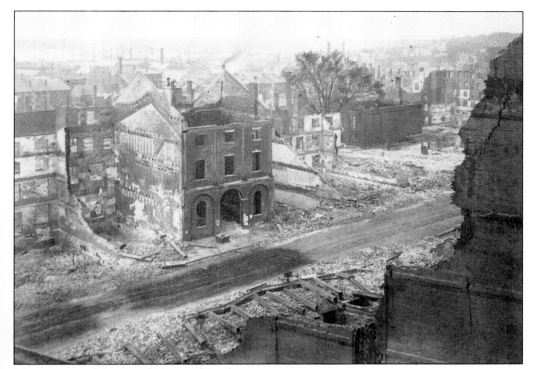

The remains of the Canal National Bank Building and part of Middle Street are shown here after the Great Fire of July 4, 1866. The bank rose again from the ashes and established a Phoenix Room in its new building.

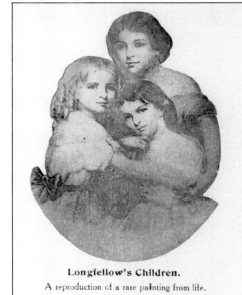

Longfellow's Children.

A reproduction of a rare painting from life.

From my study I see in the lamplight,
    Descending the great hall stair,
Grave Alice and laughing Allegra,
    And Edith with golden hair.

Longfellow

Poet Henry Wadsworth Longfellow's children are shown here, in a reproduction of a painting from life. "From my study, I see in the lamplight . . ." How many have read those words?

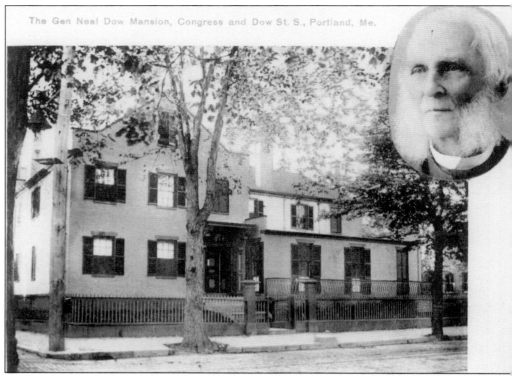

Prohibitionist Neal Dow was a general, but he is best known for getting Maine to pass a tough prohibition law.

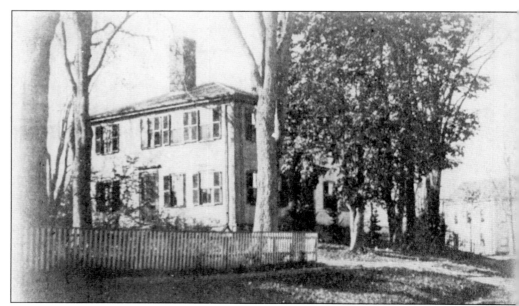

Hilltop was the Portland home of Mrs. Lillian M.N. Stevens, the national president of the Women's Christian Temperance Union (WCTU) from 1898 to 1914. She believed in keeping things dry, and must have made a powerful force when combining her efforts with those of Dow.

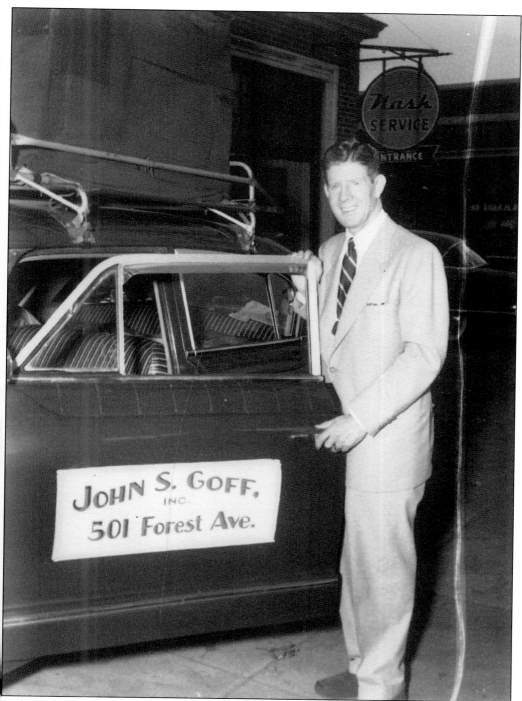

Rudy Vallee is shown here at 501 Forest Avenue, Portland, in the 1930s or '40s. Born in Vermont, Vallee grew up in Westbrook, one of Portland's neighbor cities. He was in and out of Portland a great deal after he became a singing, radio, and movie star. For years, Vallee had a palatial camp on Kezar Lake. He made the "Maine Stein Song" popular in the 1920s.

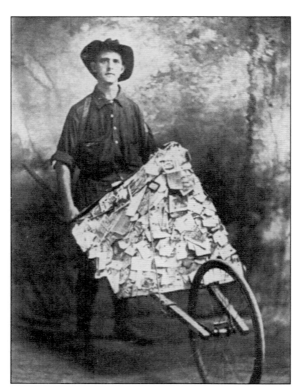

"Colonial Jack" left Portland on June 1, 1908, to walk 9,000 miles with a wheelbarrow. He went to Seattle, Los Angeles, and Jacksonville, among other places, and covered the distance in 357 days—43 days ahead of the time he had predicted he would need.

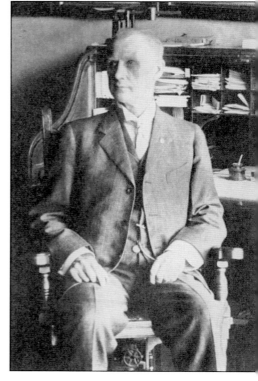

Russell G. Dyer, the grand secretary of the Independent Order of Odd Fellows, was in his Portland office when he was photographed in 1910. Dyer was grand master of the IOOF in 1890–91, and assistant grand secretary from 1896 to 1899.

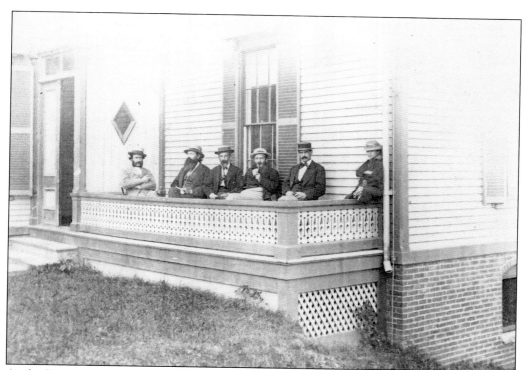

At the E.A. Noyes residence in the 1870s were, from left to right, E.A. Noyes, H.B. Brown, Charles Edwards, John Edwards, Charles E. Rolfe, and Helen A. Noyes.

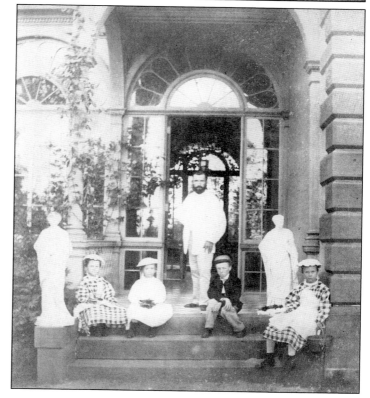

Bramhall was the J.B. Brown mansion on the Western Promenade. Brown owned a great deal of Portland business real estate.

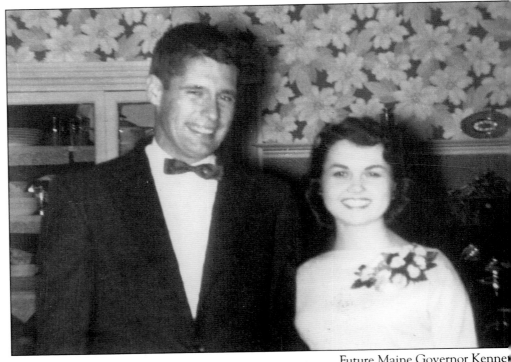

Future Maine Governor Kenne[t]
M. Curtis and his wife, the form[er]
Pauline Brown, are shown here
shortly after their 1956 marriag[e.]
The two met while working
at the Sears Roebuck store in
Portland. Curtis, after serving
as governor, became chairman
of the Democratic National
Committee, the U.S. ambassad[or]
to Canada, and president of th[e]
Maine Maritime Academy.

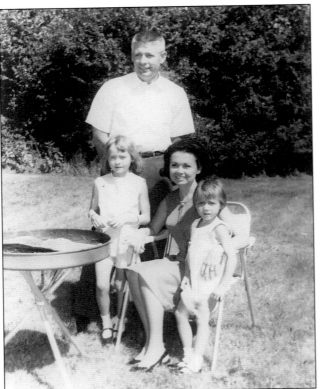

This is the Curtis' with their
two daughters, Susan (left)
and Angel. The Susan Curtis
Foundation is named after
the elder daughter, who died
while still very young.

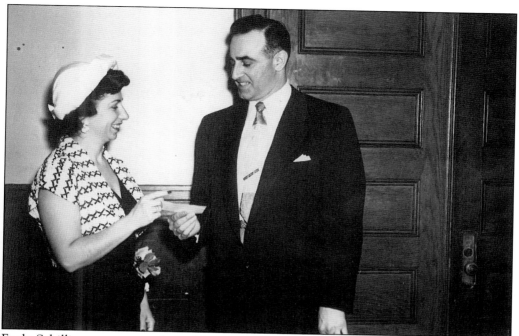

Freda Schilling presents a scholarship check to Jewish Community Center President Irving Small after the 1953 campaign to raise money for that scholarship.

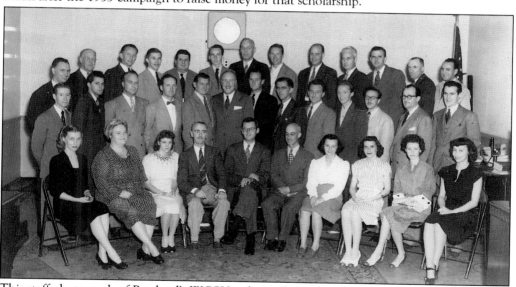

This staff photograph of Portland's WCSH radio in the early 1940s includes, from left to right: (front row) unknown, Agnes Gibbs, unknown, Bert Smith, President William Rines, Linwood Pitman, unknown, Margaret Smith, unknown, and unknown; (middle row) unknown, Eddie Lothrop, Elmer Chambers, unknown, unknown, Stan Woodman, Fred Crandon, Arthur Owens, unknown, unknown, unknown, unknown, and Wally Harwood; (back row) Tom Sawyer, Dick Lewis, Ken Cushing, unknown, Jake Brofee, unknown, Floyd Barnett, unknown, Ralph Buckley, Arthur Leavitt, George Rodick, Al Moser, and Al Reali. The photograph was taken in the WCSH radio studio in the Congress Square Hotel.

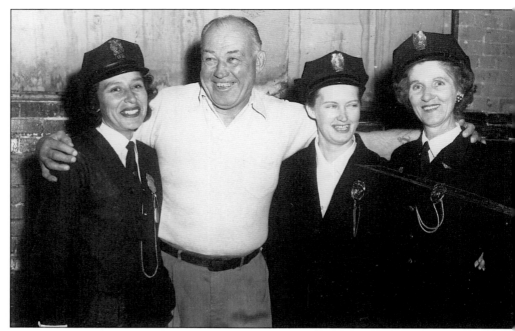

Former World Heavyweight Boxing Champion Jack Sharkey was in Portland on December 20 1958, to referee a wrestling match. A percentage of the ticket sales went to the Portland School Patrol Association. Two of those with Jack were Dolores Paquette (second from right) and Ruth Brown (far right).

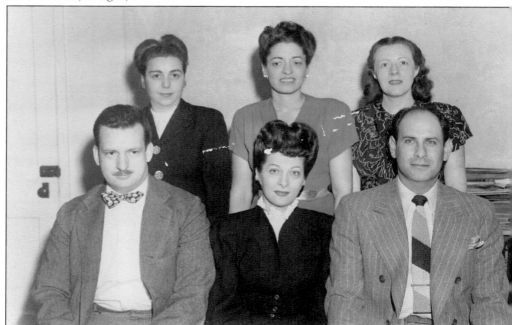

Some of those influential in the Jewish Community Center's work were, from left to right: (front row) Sumner Goffin, Dinny Cutler, and Jerry Waxman; (back row) Selma Black, Florence Halpert, and Rae Snider.

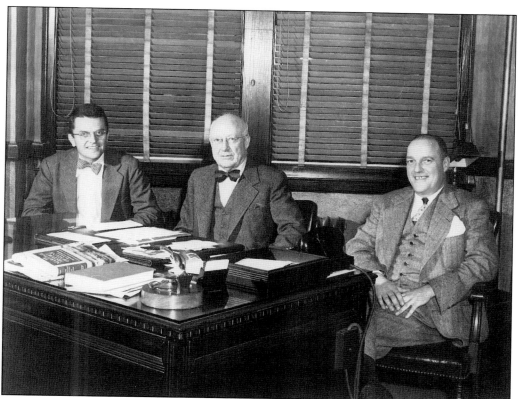

Guy P. Gannett was the founder of Guy Gannett Communications (Guy Gannett Publishing Co.). He is shown here in the early 1950s with Roger C. Williams, publisher of the Gannett newspapers, and Laurence Stubbs, general manager of those papers. Gannett purchased the *Portland Press* and the *Portland Herald* from Frederick Hale in November 1921, for a reported $195,000. He also acquired the *Evening Express* and the *Sunday Telegram*.

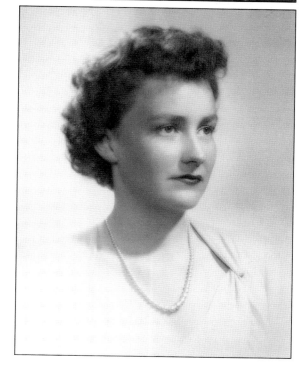

Mrs. Jean Gannett Hawley succeeded her father, Guy P. Gannett, as the publisher/owner of the Guy Gannett newspapers, television stations, and radio stations. She is shown here in the early 1950s, and was considered America's best-looking publisher/owner at that time.

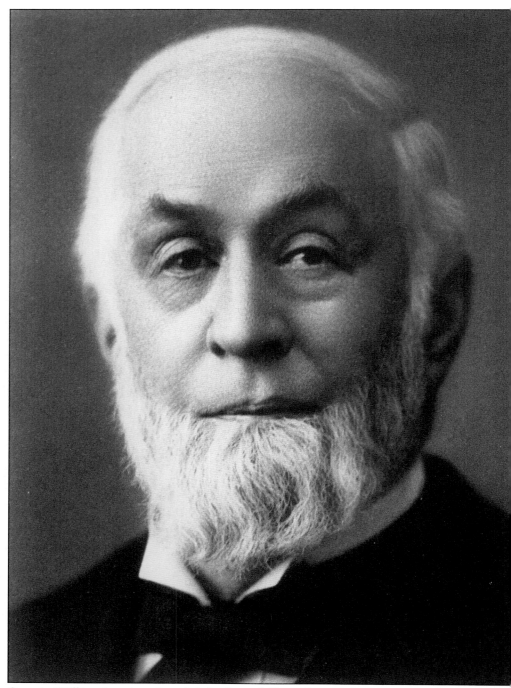

Captain William Leavitt refounded the firm of Chase, Leavitt & Co. in 1877 (his cousin ha founded it in 1856 but died at the Battle of Bull Run). William, a ship's captain by the time h was twenty-three, is part of the great tradition of Maine sea captains. He rounded Cape Horn i a full-rigged vessel, and landed in San Francisco during the Gold Rush. After his last voyage, h refounded the ship brokerage, which is now in its fifth generation on the Portland waterfront.

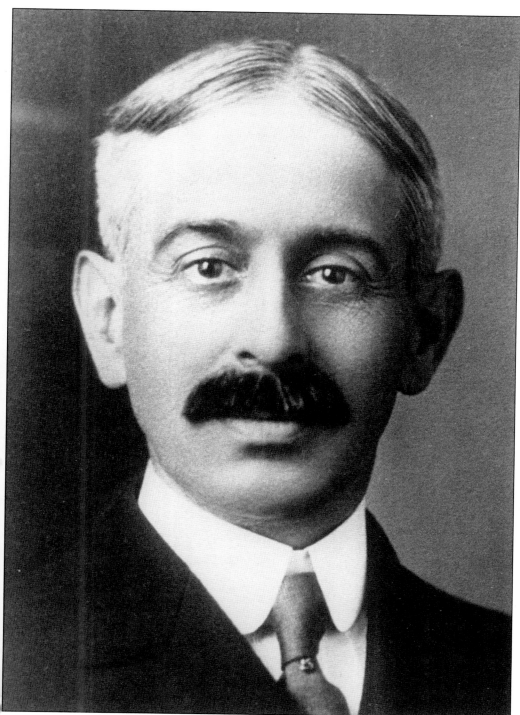

William Leavitt (1864–1926) was the second generation of Leavitts to steer the Chase, Leavitt & Co. through the tumultuous waters of the business world. The company has flourished for more than one hundred years partly because of its ability to adapt to changing conditions.

Ralph A. Leavitt (1898–1977) was a member of the third generation to run the firm. This Leavitt, to say the least, was deeply interested in politics, serving as a Republican in both the Maine House of Representatives and the Maine State Senate. He was a real doer, and founded, through legislation, both the Maine Maritime Academy and the Greater Portland Public Development Commission (which industrialized the former South Portland shipyard after World War II ended). He also founded the Portland Propeller Club, an organization of the city's waterfront interests.

William Leavitt (1928–present) is the fourth generation leader of Chase, Leavitt; his daughter Alison is the fifth generation boss. The firm continues to adapt, even to the changes of the computer age. Chase, Leavitt has provided a solid base for Portland's waterfront for years.

Five

The Waterfront

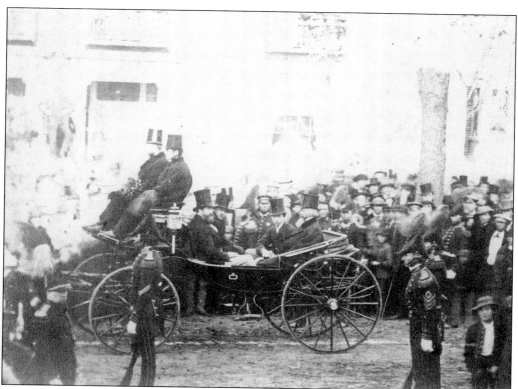

The Prince of Wales was photographed just before he departed from Portland aboard the *Hero* on October 20, 1860. In the carriage, from left to right, are: Lord Lyons, the Duke of Newcastle, the Prince, and Mayor Howard of Portland.

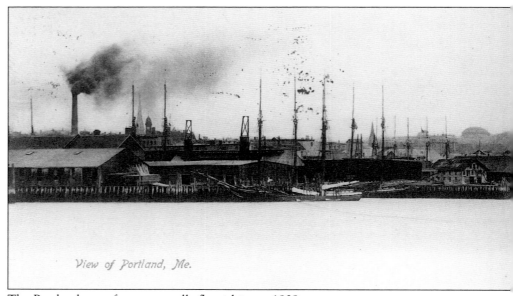

The Portland waterfront was really flourishing c. 1909.

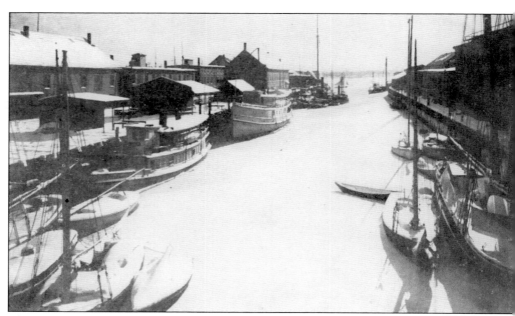

The boat landing of the Thomas Laughlin Company recovers from a snow storm on January 22, 1907.

Fort Allen, on Portland's Eastern Promenade, is shown here with two four-masters and three three-masters in Casco Bay, along with a quote from Longfellow for good measure.

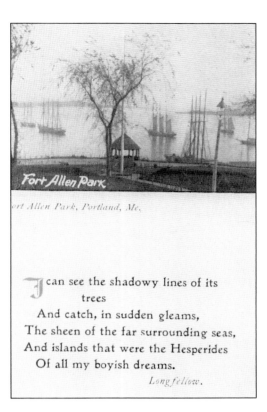

ort Allen Park, Portland, Me.

I can see the shadowy lines of its
trees
And catch, in sudden gleams,
The sheen of the far surrounding seas,
And islands that were the Hesperides
Of all my boyish dreams.

Longfellow.

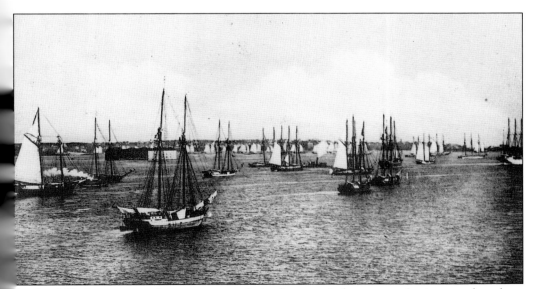

Portland Harbor recovers from a storm early in the twentieth century. Again, note how busy the waterfront was.

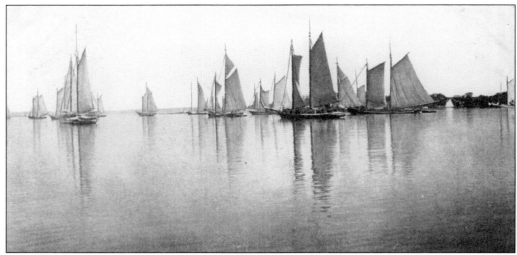

The Portland fishing fleet is shown here in harbor, just after the turn of the century. If it were not for the Portland Fish Auction, lobstering, and the catch of what were once considered junk fish, the Portland fishing fleet might have almost expired by now.

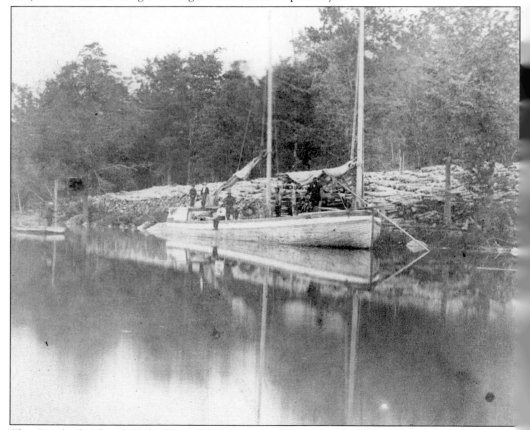

The Cumberland and Oxford Canal helped open the Portland waterfront to the interior, but i was soon superseded by railroads. This is an 1870s photograph.

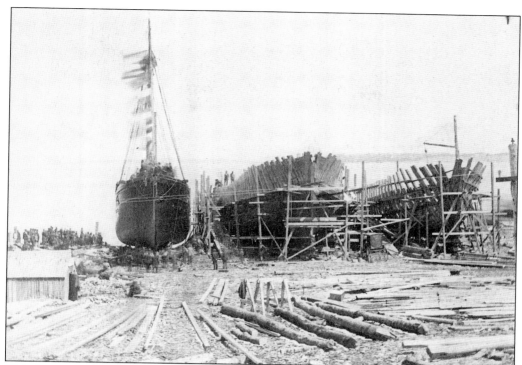

This shipyard was located below Portland's Eastern Promenade in the 1870s. Again, this was a period of great waterfront prosperity.

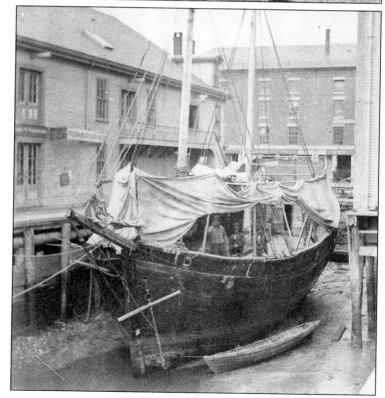

The *Ada 3* is shown here moored at the Portland Dock in the 1870s.

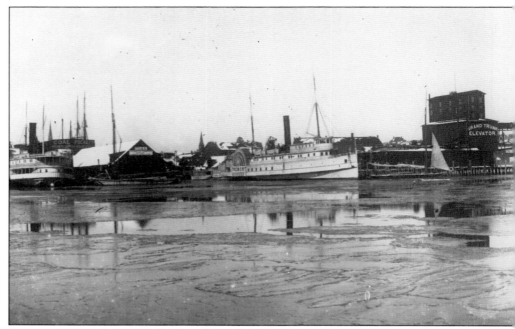

A steamer cruises by one of the Grand Trunk Railroad grain elevators on the Portland waterfron in the 1910s. All the grain elevators were eventually torn down after Portland lost its position as Canada's winter port about 1920. Parts of the last elevator to fall are now at the Samose resort in Rockport, again overlooking the sea.

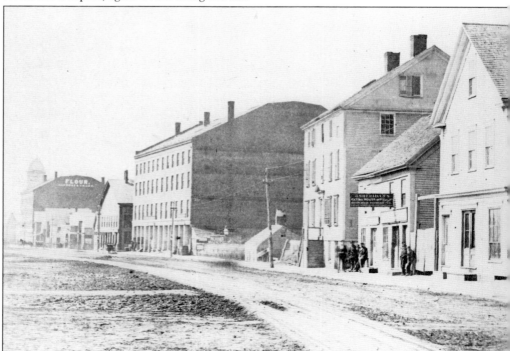

Commercial Street on the Portland waterfront is shown here in 1853, just after it was built.

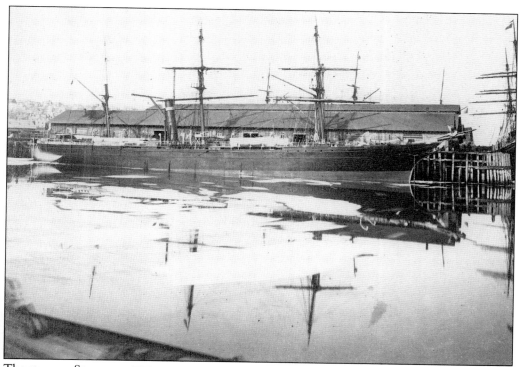

The steamer *St. Andrew* of the MOSS Company was in Portland on March 25, 1872.

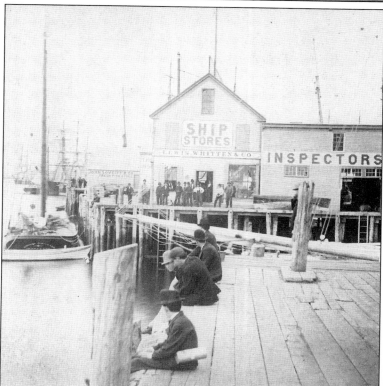

The Portland waterfront was indeed busy in the 1870s.

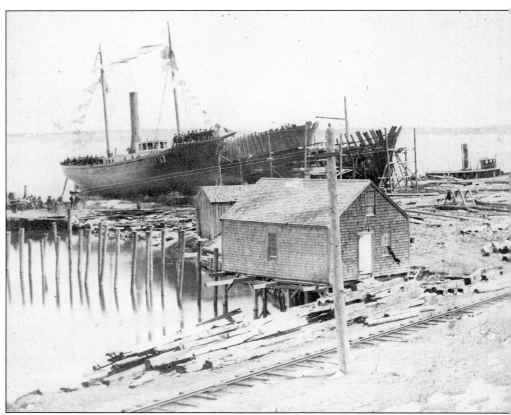

The Curtis Shipyard on Portland's Eastern Promenade is shown here in the 1870s.

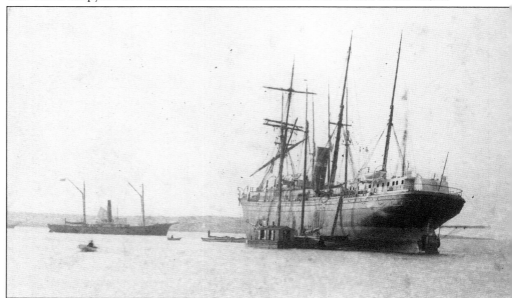

The steamship *Brooklyn* ran aground on a ledge in Portland Harbor in the 1870s. It was rigged as a barkentine.

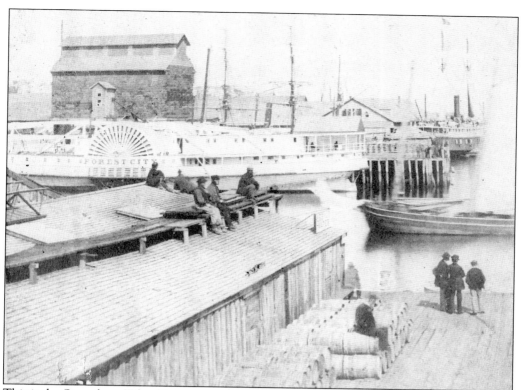

This is the Steamboat Wharf in Portland in the 1870s or '80s. The coming of the steamship, of course, revolutionized the waterfront, though sail held on for a long time.

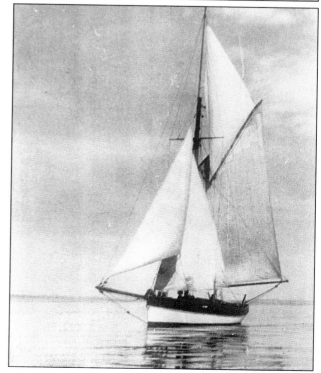

The sloop *Corineus*, modeled on English cutters, was built in 1937. Ted Langzettel, captain of the Portland Pilot boat, was lost off this sailing vessel on September 6, 1962. He was the brother of Bill Langzettel, the Associated Press correspondent in Maine for years. Bill always refused to leave this state even when given promotions elsewhere by the AP.

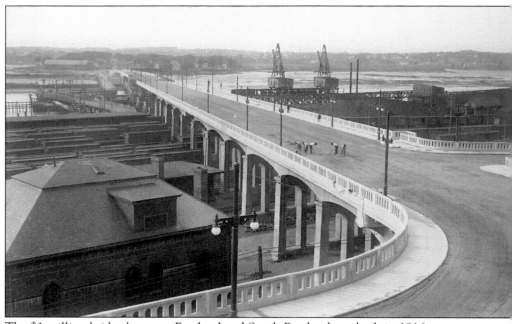

The $1 million bridge between Portland and South Portland was built in 1916.

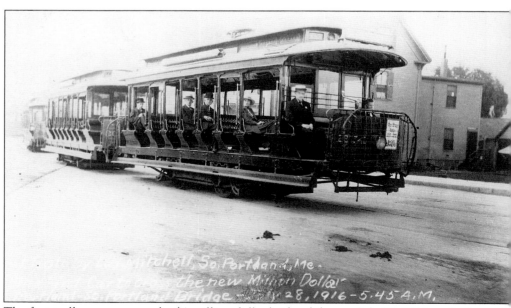

The first trolley car to cross the $1 million dollar bridge did so on July 28, 1916, at 5:45 am.

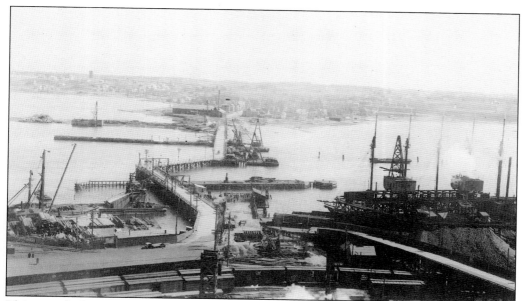

This view, looking toward South Portland, shows the temporary bridge of the early 1910s.

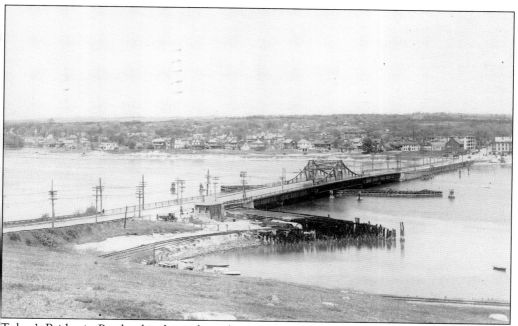

Tukey's Bridge in Portland is shown here during the 1910s or '20s.

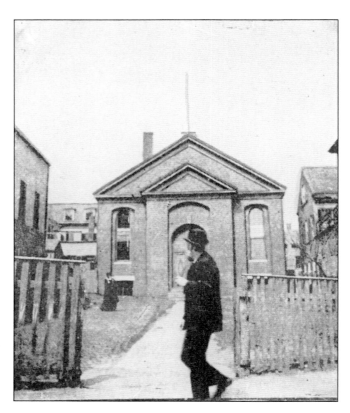

The Italian Mission was located at the Mariners' Bethel, 284 Fore Street, about 1909. There were various agencies and charitable organizations to help sailors in distress while in port.

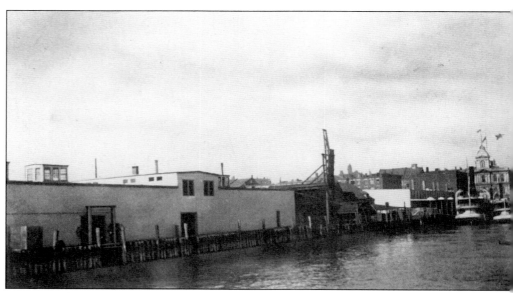

Steamers of the Harpswell Line can be seen in this view looking toward the Custom House in the 1910s or '20s.

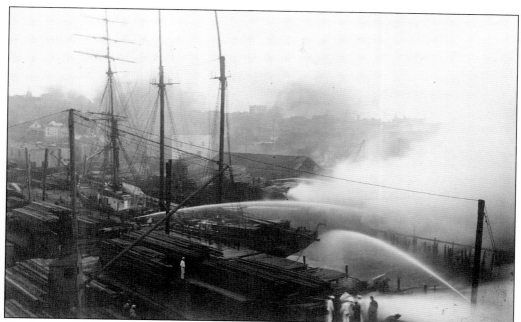

The damage caused by this pre-1912 fire paled in comparison to that caused by the Fire of 1866. The blaze can be seen just beyond the three-masted vessel on the left.

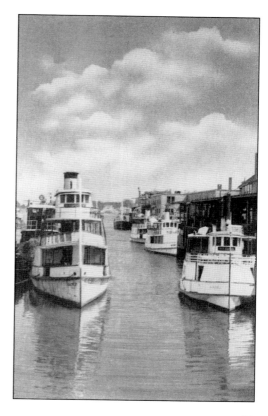

Casco Bay Lines connected Portland with the islands of Casco Bay in the 1950s and later.

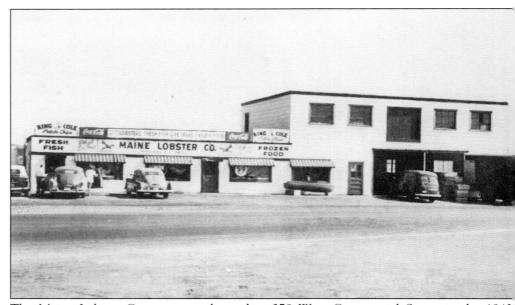

The Maine Lobster Company was located at 378 West Commercial Street in the 1940s. Lobstering eventually became the highest cash crop harvested from the waters off the coast of Maine.

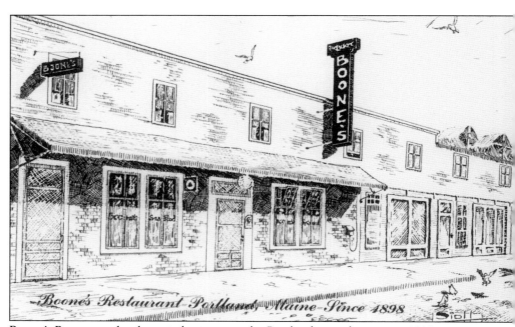

Boone's Restaurant has been in business on the Portland waterfront since 1898.

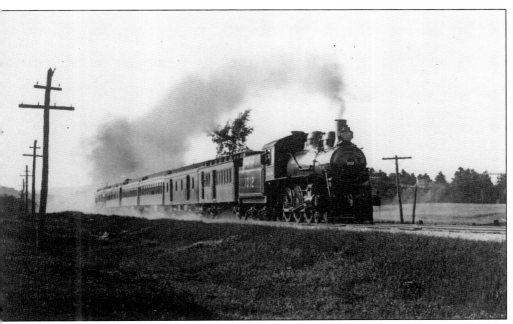

Grand Trunk Railroad engine No. 2 ran from Chicago to the Portland waterfront at 55 miles an hour in the 1940s.

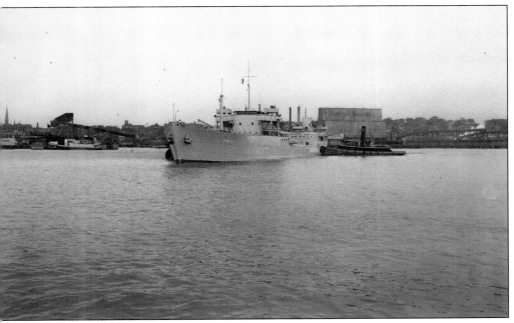

A tug boat nudges a vessel in Portland Harbor in the 1930s.

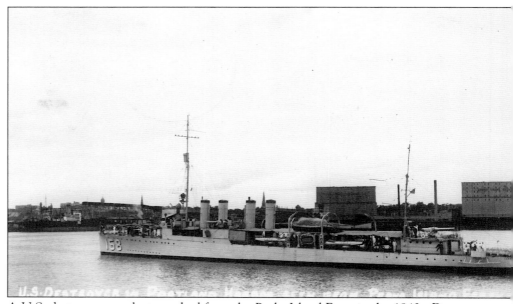

A U.S. destroyer was photographed from the Peaks Island Ferry in the 1940s. Destroyers were invaluable in protecting convoys from enemy submarines.

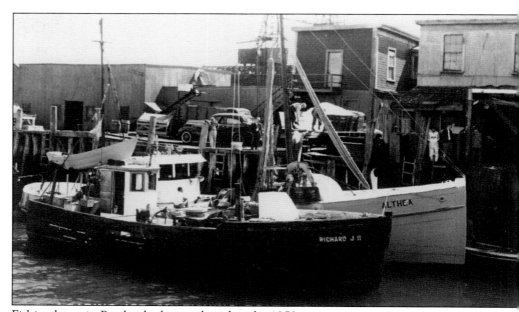

Fishing boats in Portland take ice aboard in the 1950s.

Six

Leisure and Sports

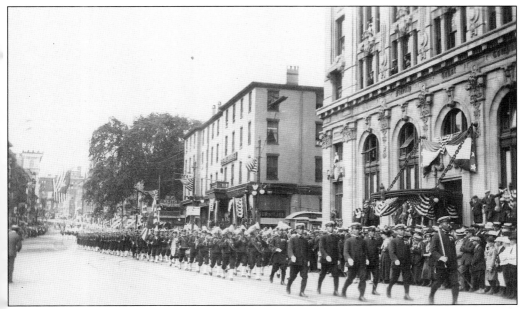

The Maine Centennial Celebration Parade on Congress Street was photographed on July 5, 1920, as it passed the Fidelity Building. Parades were an important part of leisure time in Portland.

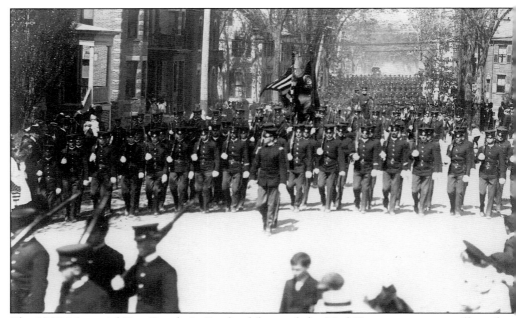

The 1909 Memorial Day Parade in Portland featured the 23rd Company, coast artillery, from Fort McKinley.

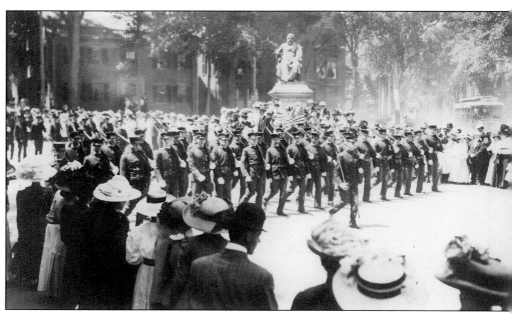

Uniformed men march by the Longfellow Square statue of the famed poet during the 1910 Fourth of July Parade.

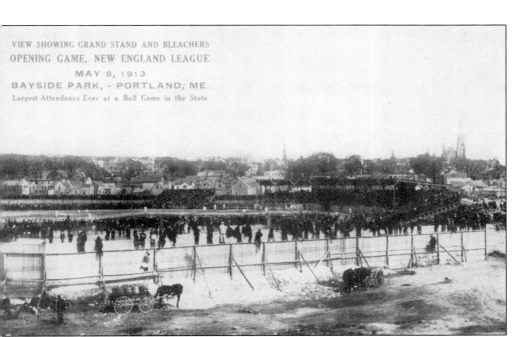

VIEW SHOWING GRAND STAND AND BLEACHERS
OPENING GAME, NEW ENGLAND LEAGUE
MAY 8, 1913
BAYSIDE PARK, - PORTLAND, ME.
Largest Attendance Ever at a Ball Game in the State

This view shows the grandstand and bleachers at the opening game of the New England League in Portland's Bayside Park on May 8, 1913. The 8,300 people who attended constituted the largest crowd at a ball game in Portland up until that time. Unfortunately, the visiting team from Lowell, Massachusetts, won.

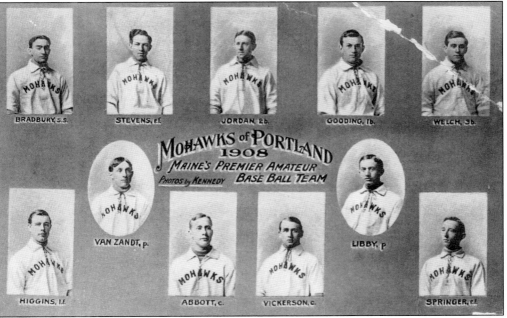

The 1908 Mohawks of Portland were "Maine's premier amateur baseball team." Players included Bradbury (shortstop), Stevens (center field), Jordan (second base), Gooding (first base), Welch (third base), Higgins (left field), Van Zandt (pitcher), Abbott (catcher), Vickerson (catcher), Libby (pitcher), and Springer (right field).

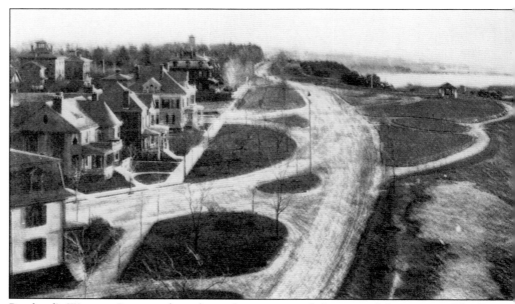

Portland's Western Promenade is shown here at around the turn of the century. The Eastern and Western Promenades were created in the late 1830s.

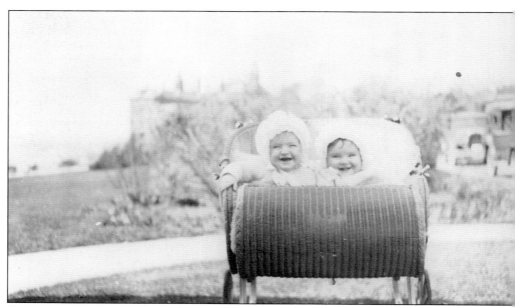

Twin sisters Katherine Elizabeth Owen and Margaret Shurtleff Owen were photographed on the Eastern Promenade in May 1928.

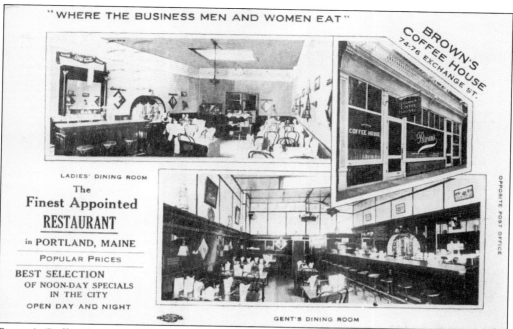

Brown's Coffee House was located at 74–76 Exchange Street in the 1900s, and was "Where the Business Men and Women Eat." It had both a ladies and a gents dining room and called itself "The finest appointed restaurant in Portland, Maine." It was open night and day and boasted of "the best selection of noon-day specials in the city."

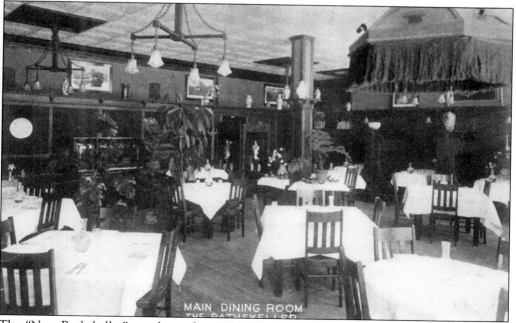

The "New Rathskeller" was located at 12–14 Brown Street in the 1900s. It was one of the city's best-known restaurants, and featured a banquet hall, a main dining room, and two smaller dining rooms. To top it all off, there was orchestra music every evening.

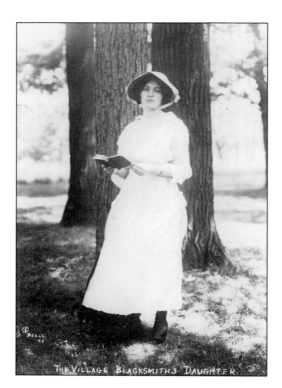

The Village Blacksmith's Daughter

Mrs. Lowe was the village blacksmith's daughter in the 1913 Fourth of July Portland Pageant.

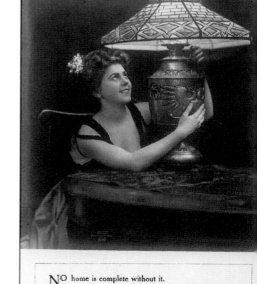

The F.H. Little Oil Company of Portland used advertisements featuring a girl with a lamp: "No home is complete without it. A well-kept Lamp filled with FIRESIDE OIL gives perfect illumination, safety and comfort. We have the oil; the rest is easy. Just try it. Do it now!"

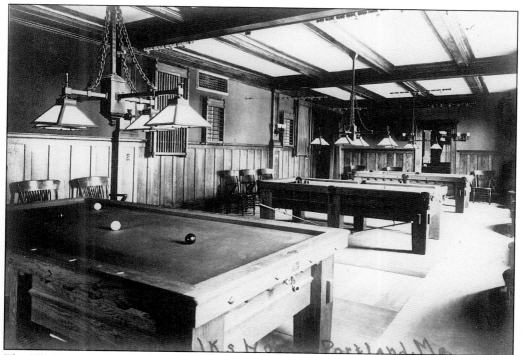

The Elks Home in Portland with its billiard tables is shown here in the 1910s.

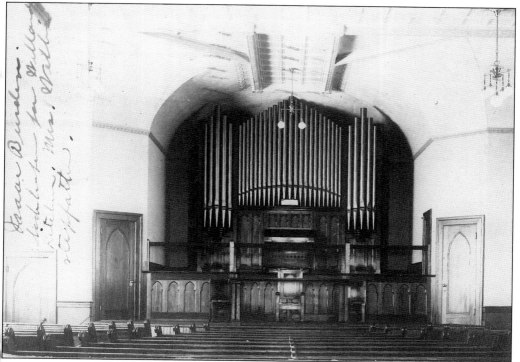

This organ is in a Portland church, possibly the Williston West Church.

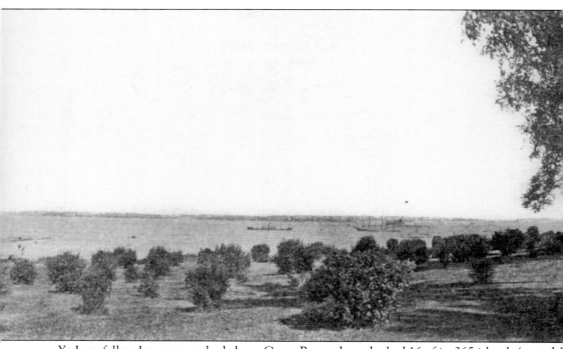

Ye Longfellow Inn was perched above Casco Bay and overlooked 16 of its 365 islands (a myth).
The impressive inn was located at 130 Eastern Promenade in the 1910s. It was 108 feet abov

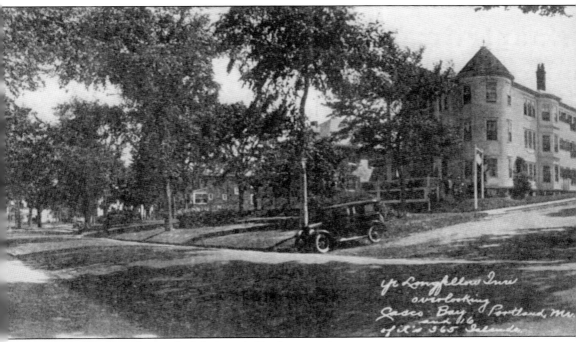

Ye Longfellow Inn
overlooking
Casco Bay, Portland, Me.
and 116
of it's 365 Islands.

sea level, and had a truly wonderful view. A. Forsberg was its manager.

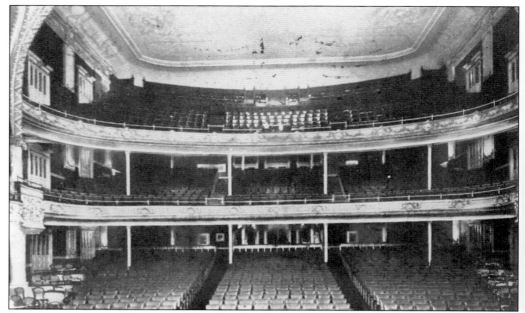

This photograph of the auditorium was taken from the stage of Keith's new theater about 1908.

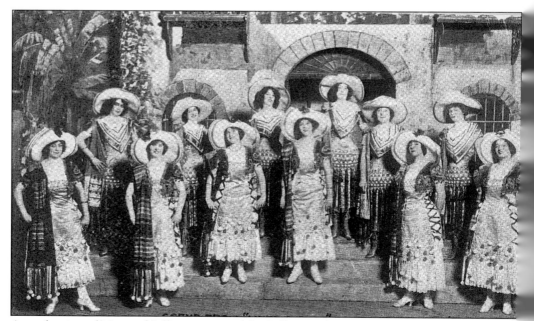

A production of *Mutt and Jeff* was put on at the Jefferson Theater on February 2 in the 1910s o '20s. The show was said to have been successful in New York, Chicago, and Boston. Portlan was a theater town, partly because of the success enjoyed by summer theaters all along the coas of Maine.

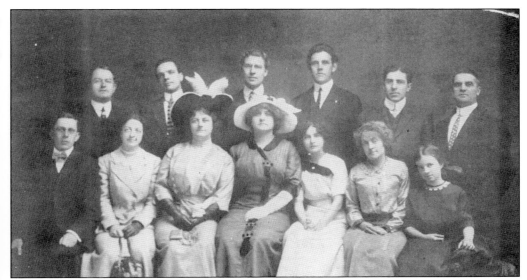

These members of Portland's B.F. Keith Stock Company, *c.* 1910, were, from left to right: (front row) Ralph Lingley; Mrs. James Moore; Billy D'arcy; Adelaide Keirn; unknown; ? Craig; and Mrs. Moore's daughter; (back row) James Albion; unknown; Adelaide Keirn's husband; Sidney Toler, who later went on to fame as Charlie Chan; James Lawrence; and James Moore.

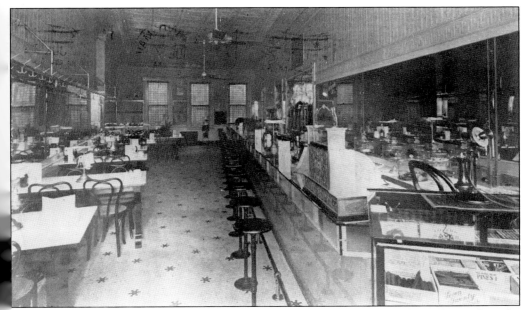

The Astor Cafe was located at 18 Temple Street, a few doors above the Falmouth Hotel, in the 1910s. It claimed to be "Maine's Finest and Most Sanitary" restaurant and lunch place. Charles E. Rowse was the manager. It had private dining rooms and ladies dining rooms, as well as featuring homemade pastry and Hotel Astor coffee.

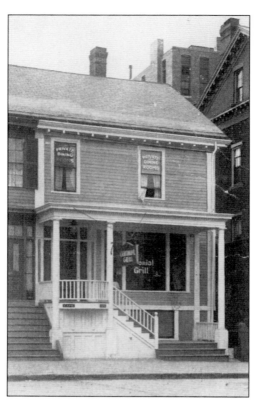

Colonial Grill, at 595 Congress Street, claimed to be the "only up-to-date Bohemian Cafe for ladies and gentlemen east of Boston." This was in the 1900s. Specialties included planked steaks, broiled lives (assumed to mean lobsters), and Chinese dishes.

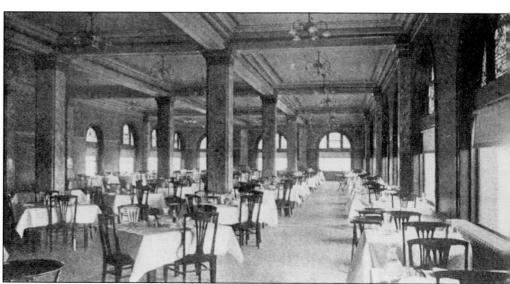

The dining hall at the Congress Square Hotel is shown here in the 1900s. The hotel was owned by the Rines family, which also owned the Rines Bros. store and Walnut Crest Farm in nearby Gorham. The hotel featured dairy products, poultry, lamb, and vegetables from Walnut Crest Farm, and an advertisement states that Rines took great care with his herd, which was "one of the few in the state" to withstand federal government tests without loss or criticism.

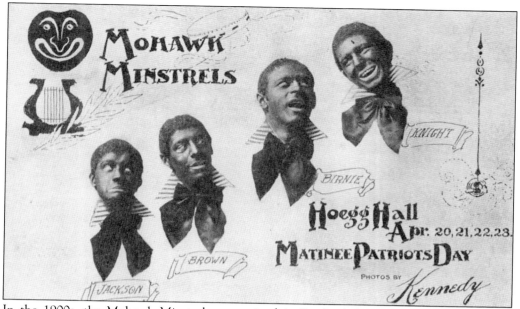

In the 1900s, the Mohawk Minstrels entertained in Portland from April 20 to 23, with a matinee on Patriots' Day. They included Jackson, Brown, Bernie, and Knight, and performed at Hoegg Hall.

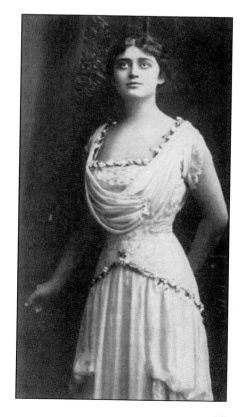

Famed soprano Alma Gluck sang at the Maine Music Festival in Portland from October 10 to 12, 1910.

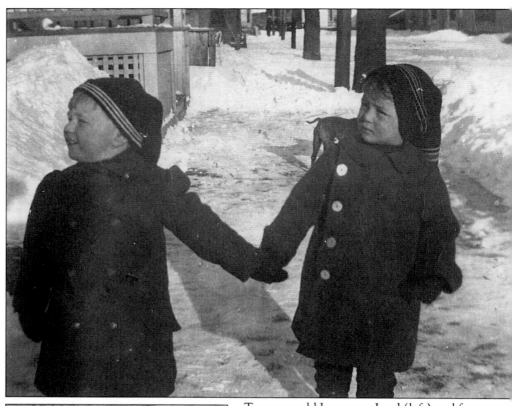

Two-year-old Lawrence Lord (left) and four-year-old Preston Leavitt take a leisurely stroll in 1905 on Vaughn Street in Portland.

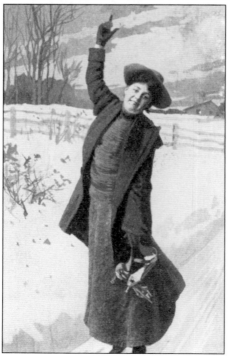

This young woman in the winter was an advertisement for Hinds' Honey and Almond Cream, which was made in Portland in the 1900s.

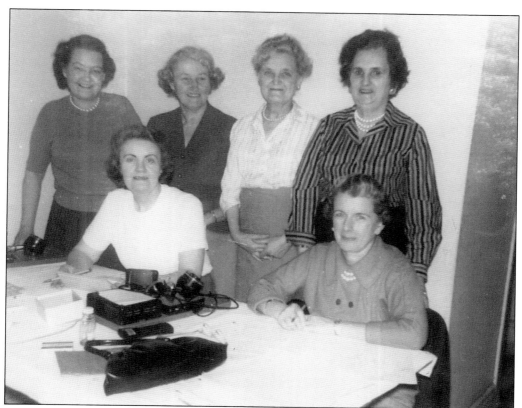

Lucia Miles, Gertrude Forbes, Dorothy Hersey, Adelaide Koontz, Pauline Martin, and Elizabeth Rafferty were volunteers at the Portland office of the Maine Cancer Society in 1961. The picture was taken by Lillian McKinnon.

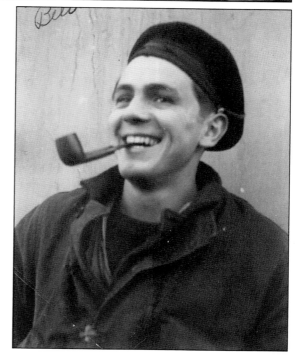

Andre Bellier, a French sailor, is shown here at the USO on Pearl Street in February 1944, during World War II.

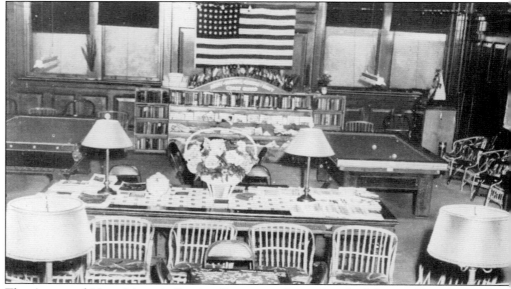

The Army and Navy Masonic Service Center was located in the Masonic Temple, Portland during World War II. The U.S. Marine Corps and Coast Guard were also covered.

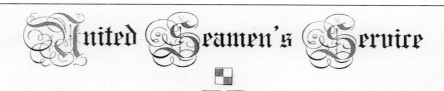

United Seamen's Service

AWARD OF MERIT TO

Kitty Forbes

Who, with patriotic and unselfish devotion, worked as a Volunteer in the United Seamen's Service and thus encouraged American Merchant Seamen to man the great Merchant Fleet which carried the supplies of Victory to every fighting front in World War II. This Certificate is awarded in grateful recognition and appreciation of these services.

E S Land
Chairman of the Board

Wm S. Newell
President

OCTOBER 28, 1945

On October 28, 1945, Kitty Forbes (now Mrs. Catherine Carswell) was given an award of meri in recognition of her volunteer work in the United Seamen's Service, the Merchant Marine. I was signed by William S. (Pete) Newell, the president of Bath Iron Works.

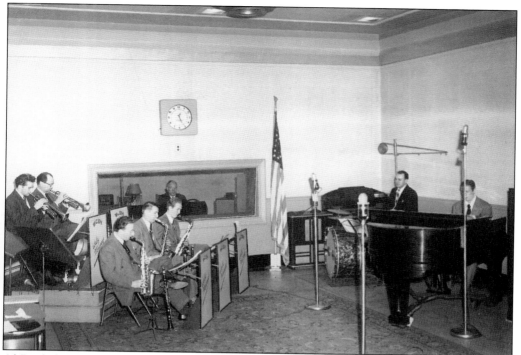

Al Reali (on the drums, second from right) was a member of Wally Harwood's WCSH studio band in the 1940s.

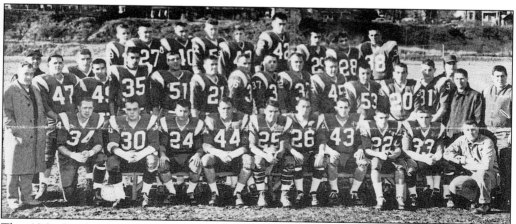

The 1961 Portland Sea Hawks were the New England semi-pro football champions after defeating Whitman (Massachusetts), 6–0. From left to right are: (first row) Dennis Perry, Rudy Rutherford, Willie Greenlaw, Tom Meehan, team captain Jerry Davis, Ken Parady, Mike DeSimon, Tom Delaney, Ronnie Estes, and business manager George Cadigan; (middle row) Charlie Kilbride, Jess Cook, Hal (Tank) Violette, Dick Daniels, John Pompeo, Frank Johnson, Dave Berman, Tom Vail, Richie Ashley, Louie Drouin, Al Chretian, Bill Bath, Andre Lestage, Art Gonyea, Steve Linsky, Thomas Walsh, Sonny Noel, and Coach Bill Amergian; (back row) George Rockwell, Bill Gagne, Frank Nadeau, Jack Norton, Bill Cummings, John Dinan, Pee Wee DeSarno, Tony DiPietro, and Bob Bragg.

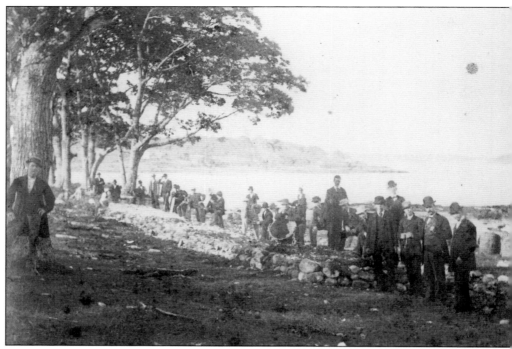

The ruins of a clam bake tell of the mighty appetites at a Masonic celebration on June 24, 1879.

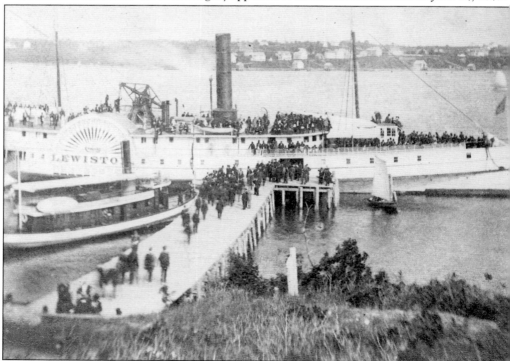

The steamer *Lewiston* was quite a ship. She is shown here docked on the same day that the photograph at the top of the page was taken.

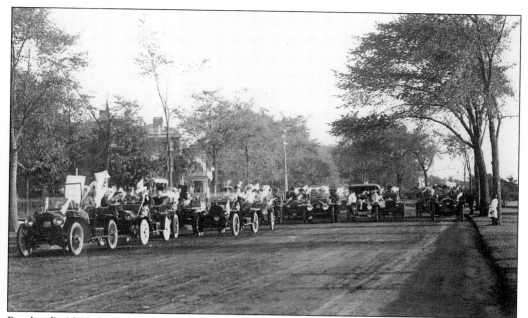

Portland's 1910 Auto Parade was an electrifying event.

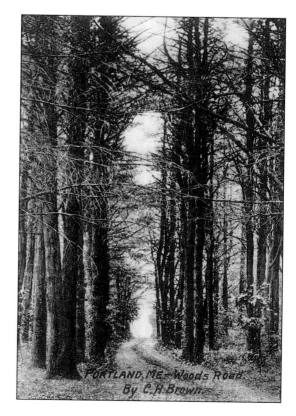

What could be more peaceful than one of Portland's wooded roads in the early 1900s?

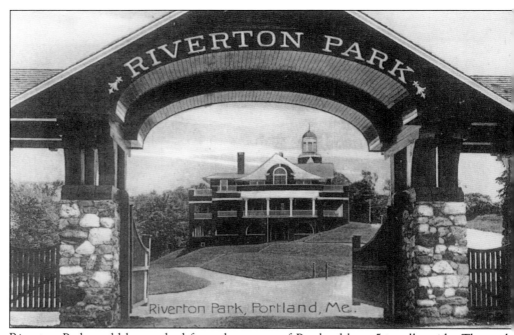

Riverton Park could be reached from the center of Portland by a 5¢ trolley ride. The park casino can be seen through the entrance.

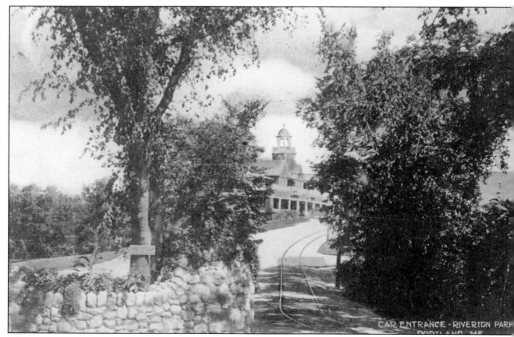

The trolley car entrance to Riverton Park is shown here in the 1900s. The trolley company built the park to attract more customers.

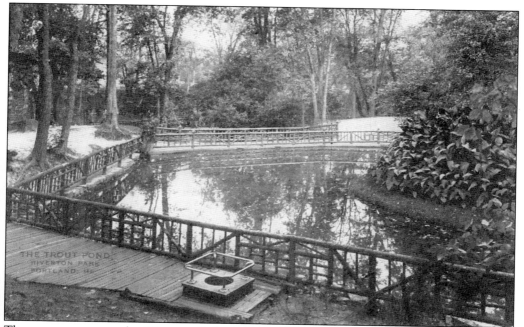

There was a trout pond at Riverton Park in the 1900s.

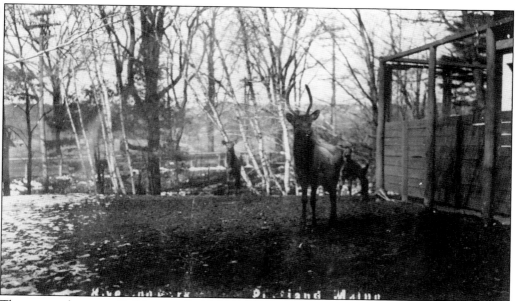

There were deer as well. Riverton Park was a family park with much for children to do and see.

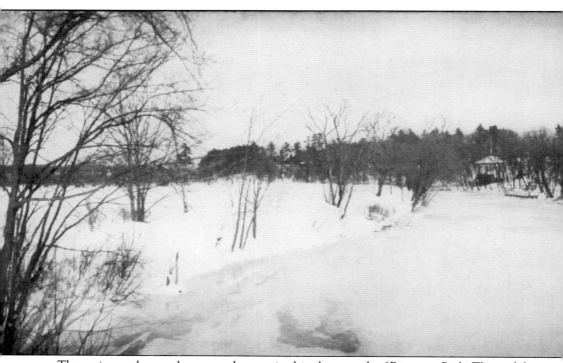

The casino and canoe house can be seen in this photograph of Riverton Park. The park has now disappeared except for parts of its entrance. There have been a few sporadic efforts to reviv

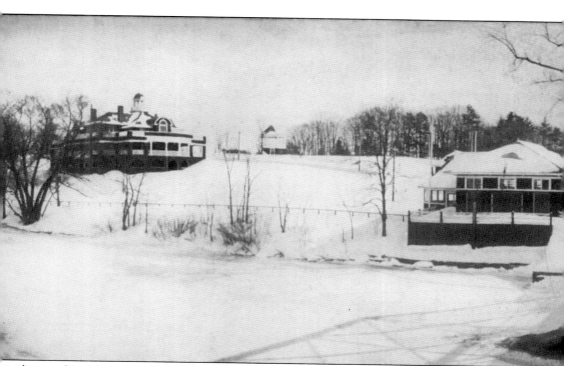

it, but to this point, none have succeeded. Of course, there are now no trolleys in Portland. Children especially were impressed by the entertainments the park had to offer.

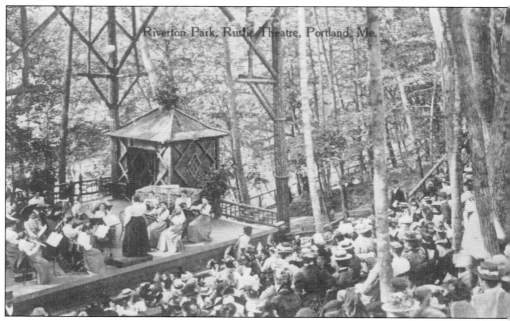

Riverton Park's rustic theater packed people in.

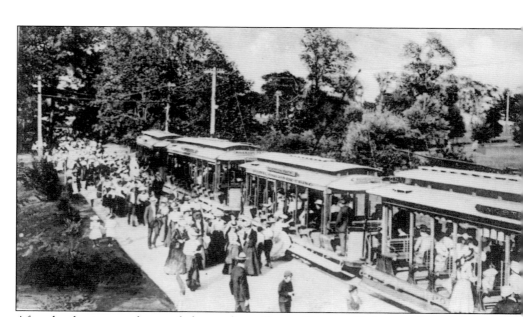

After the theater people crowded onto the trolleys at Riverton Park to catch a ride home.

Seven

Congress Street

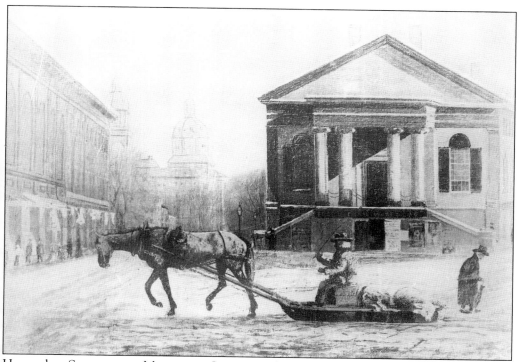

Haymarket Square, now Monument Square, is shown here in 1869, with Congress Street running through its center.

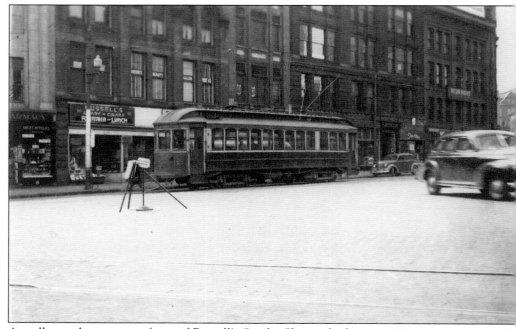

A trolley and cars are in front of Russell's Smoke Shop, which was in Monument Square for years. The date is April 6, 1941—a time when Congress Street was at its busiest.

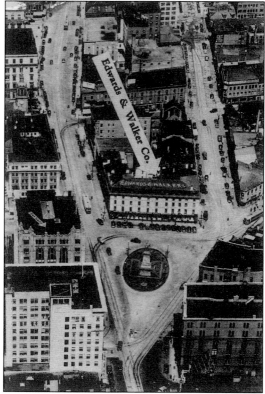

This 1940s bird's-eye view shows the Edwards and Walker hardware store (once the United States Hotel) and Monument Square. The Edwards and Walker building was razed to make way for new buildings. The center of Portland had no new buildings erected from 1928 to the 1960s, largely because of the depression.

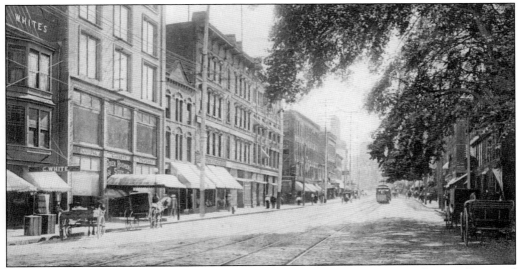

Congress Street was usually very busy in the 1900s. This was a time when trolleys and automobiles shared the roads.

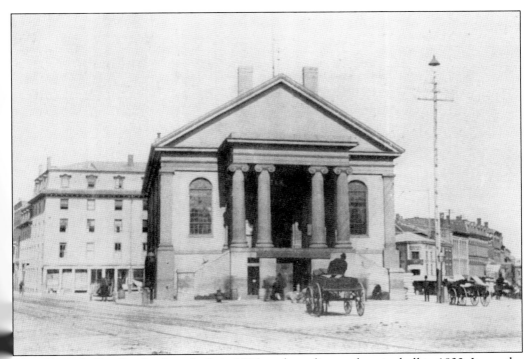

The old city hall in Portland was built in 1825, and was first used as city hall in 1832. It was the scene of a rum riot in 1854, and was demolished in 1888. The Soldiers and Sailors Monument in Monument Square now stands on its site.

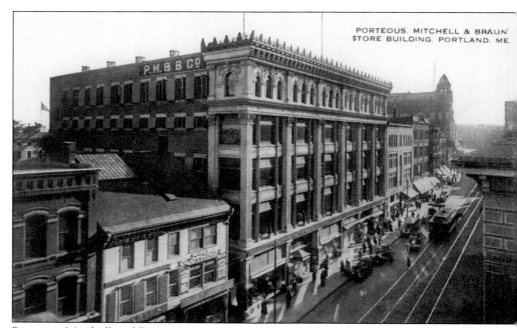

Porteous, Mitchell and Braun Co. was Congress Street's largest department store in 1916. Joh Porteous purchased the Miller Building on Congress Street in 1906.

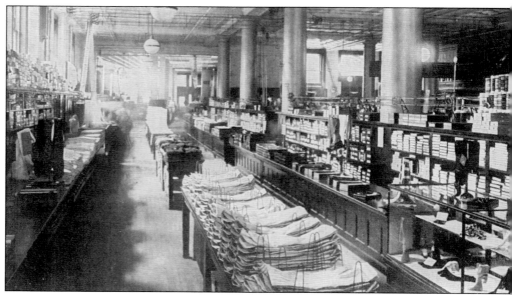

This is the main aisle at Porteous, Mitchell and Braun in the 1910s. It had class.

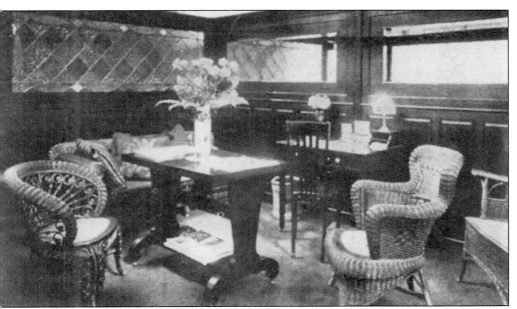

Owen, Moore and Company, at 505–507 Congress Street, was another bulwark of Maine's largest business hub. It billed itself as "the largest specialty store" east of Boston, and it was that. This is the ladies rest room.

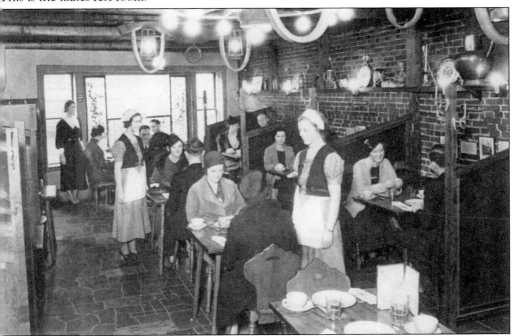

It was said that "the restful atmosphere of old Holland" prevailed at the Oxbow Room of the Dutch coffee shop at 588A Congress Street. The shop could also be reached through the H.H. Hay Drug Store, and it had more than one hundred seats, twenty-one of them by the windows. Ten "smiling Dutch maids," all from Portland, were the waitresses. This photograph was taken in the 1920s or '30s.

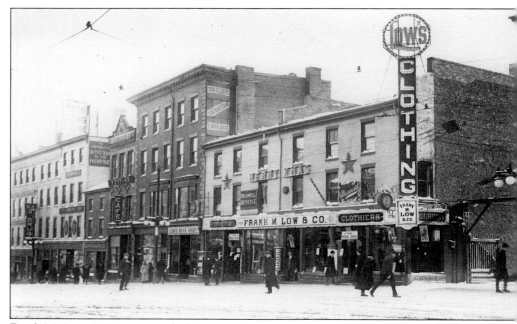

Frank M. Low & Company, clothiers, was located at Monument Square and Middle Street in the 1910s. It was eventually purchased by the A.H. Benoit Company.

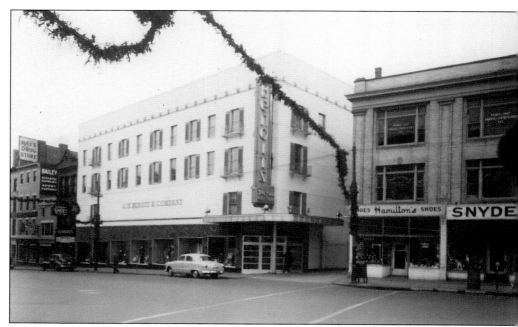

The A.H. Benoit Company is shown here in the 1950s at Monument Square. At this time it was probably Maine's leading mens clothing store.

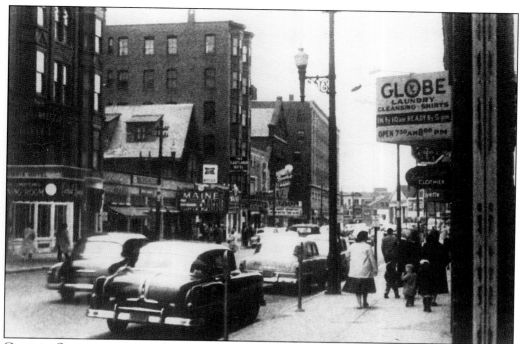

Congress Street was at one of its business peaks in the late 1930s and early 1940s. The Maine and Capitol Theaters no longer exist, nor does Globe Laundry. The Columbia Hotel (in the left foreground) is now a University of Southern Maine dormitory. The basic challenge is to find new uses for many of the buildings on what used to be Maine's busiest business street.

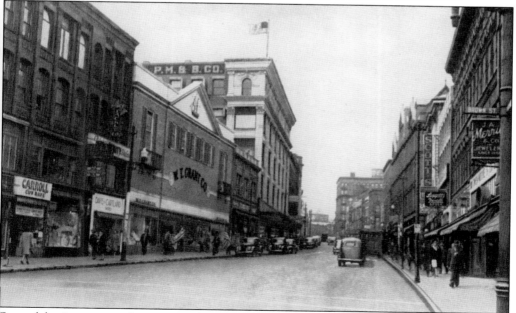

Several businesses can be seen in this view of a flourishing Congress Street in the 1940s, including W.T. Grant, Carroll Cut Rate, J.A. Merrill, Liggett's Drug Store, Davis & Cartland Shoes, and Scott's.

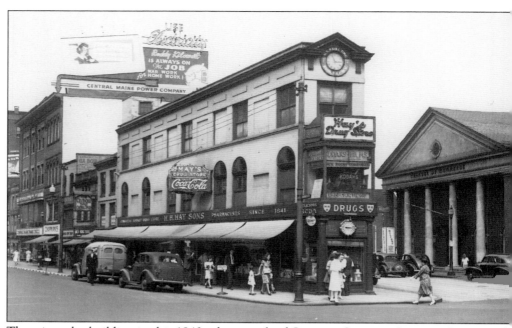

The triangular building in this 1940s photograph of Congress Street at Congress Square is the H.H. Hay Drug Store. It's been a landmark ever since it was built.

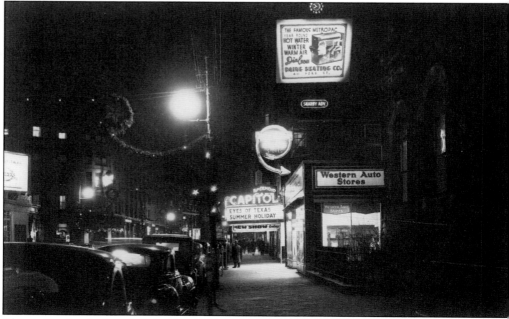

This is Portland after dark in the 1940s. The Capitol Theater is showing *Eyes of Texas* and *Summer Holiday*.

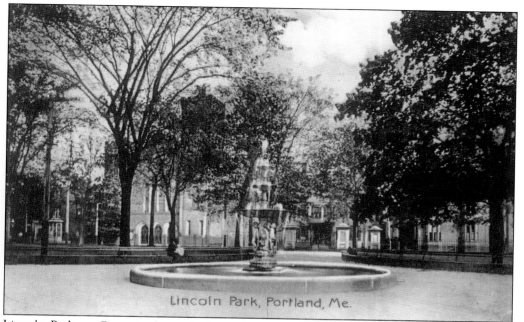

Lincoln Park on Congress Street is shown here at the turn of the century. The park is still there today.

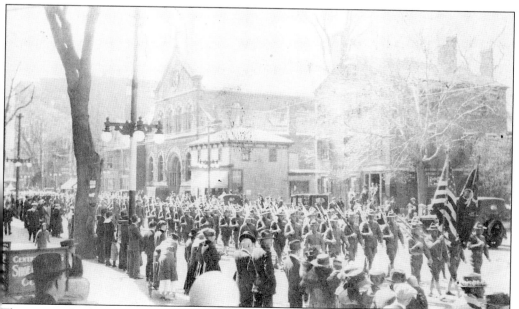

This postcard, of Congress Street in front of the Portland Public Library, is dated November 5, 1918, six days before the Armistice ended World War I.

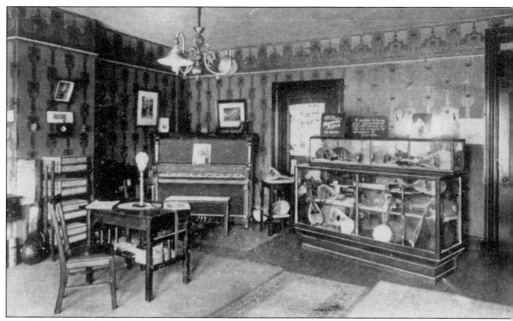

Clifford E. Leighton was a teacher of the mandolin; this is the interior of his studio at 548 1/2 Congress Street. It's just a bit of what went on inside some of the Congress Street buildings.

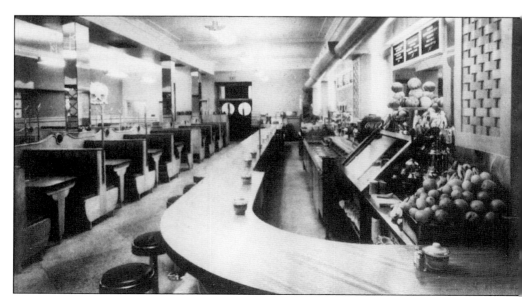

The Blaine Restaurant was located at 572 Congress Street in the 1930s.

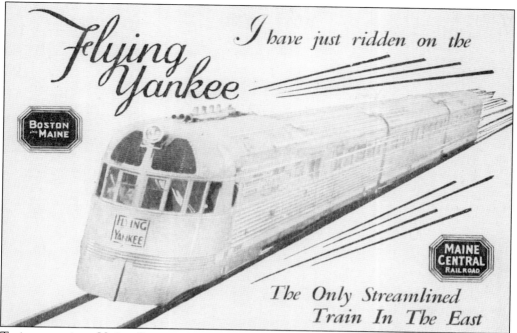

Trains came in at Union Station, near Congress Street. This is the streamlined Flying Yankee, which made fast, comfortable trips from Boston to Bangor and back for the Boston & Maine Railroad in the mid and late 1930s. The Flying Yankee was built in 1935.

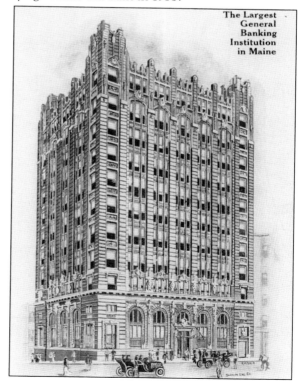

The Fidelity Building on Congress Street in Monument Square was recently purchased by Mrs. Elizabeth Noyce. It is shown here in the 1910s.

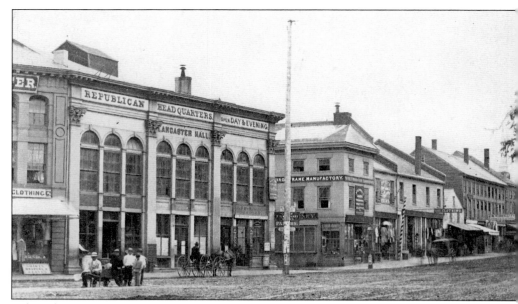

Politics have always been a part of Congress Street, whether in the form of political headquarters, people talking politics, or people giving speeches in Monument Square. Lancester Hall (shown here) held the Republican headquarters sometime in the 1870s or '80s.

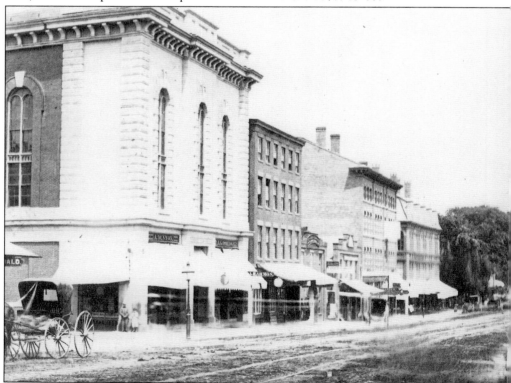

Mechanics Hall on Congress Street is shown here in the 1870s or '80s from the corner of Congress and Casco Streets. The Wadsworth-Longfellow House is under the trees at the right.

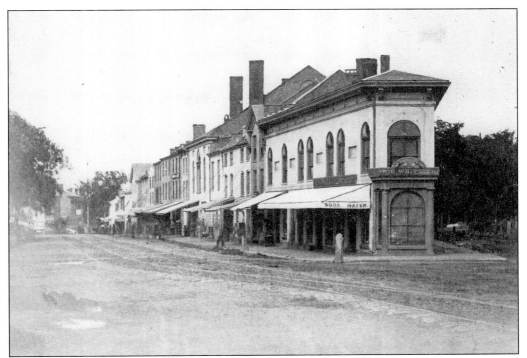

Congress Street below High Street was captured in this nineteenth-century photograph.

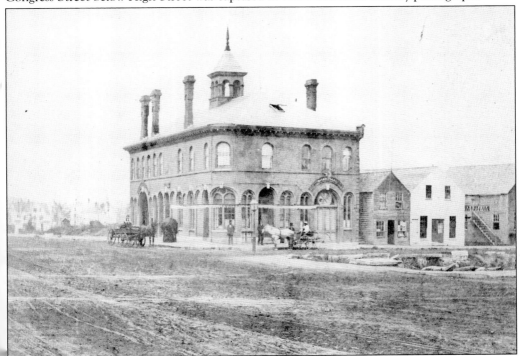

The City Fire Engine House on Congress Street was photographed before the Great Fire of July 4, 1866.

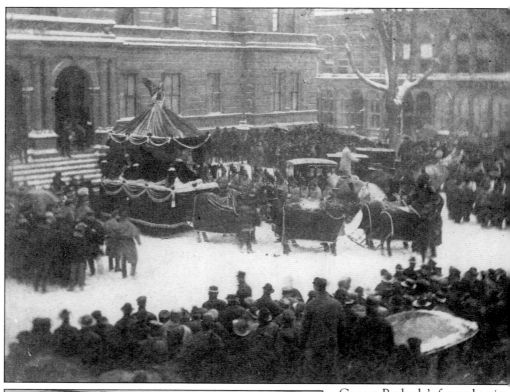

George Peabody's funeral train is shown here in a photograph taken from Portland City Hall in the 1890s.

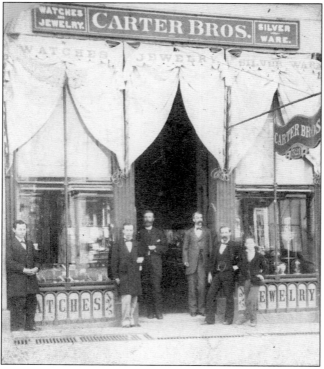

Carter Bros. on Congress Street sold watches, jewelry, and silverware. This was another long-lived Congress Street business.

This is the president's room of the Union Mutual Life Insurance Company (now UNUM) headquarters, located on Congress Street.

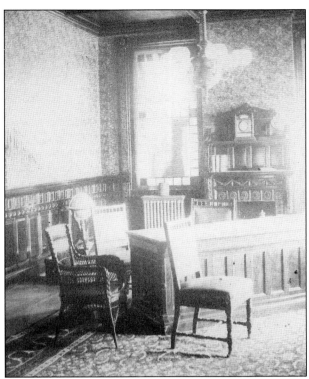

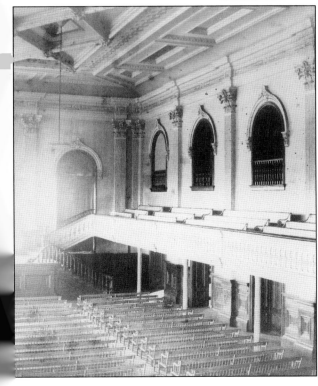

The Portland City Hall Auditorium is shown here in the 1870s.

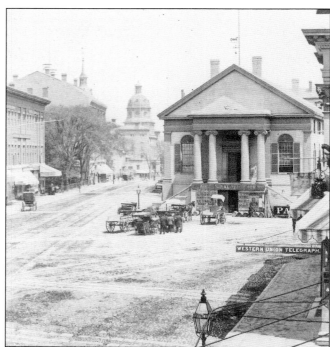

This photograph of Haymarket Square (now Monument Square) on Congress Street was taken on September 9, 1879.

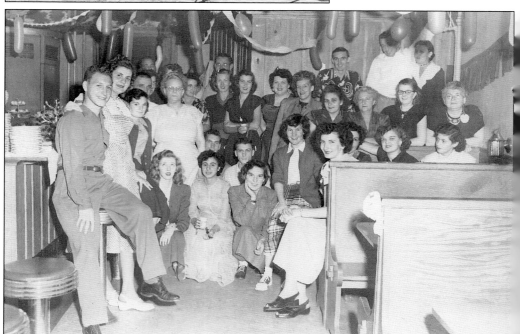

It is believed John Mayo, the owner of Your Host Restaurant on Congress Street, took this photograph of a Christmas Party at the restaurant in 1950 or 1951. Among those shown are Dale and Frances Harris, Mr. and Mrs. Don Mayo (John's brother), Mrs. John Mayo, Cecile Pelletier, Kelly Hawkes, Millard and Mary Moody, Evelyn Sanborn (Scribner), Mary Gillespie, Marian Bellefontaine, Mary and Dottie Butler, and Theresa Gillespie.

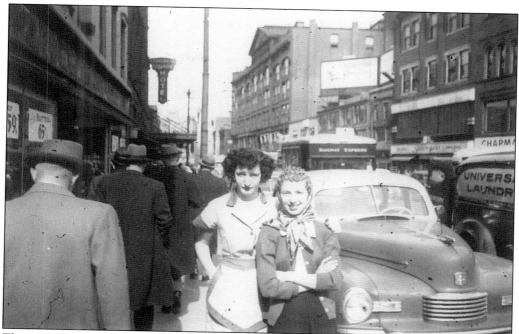

Theresa Gillespie (Ganem) and Evelyn Sanborn (Scribner) are shown here on a busy Congress Street in 1950 or 1951.

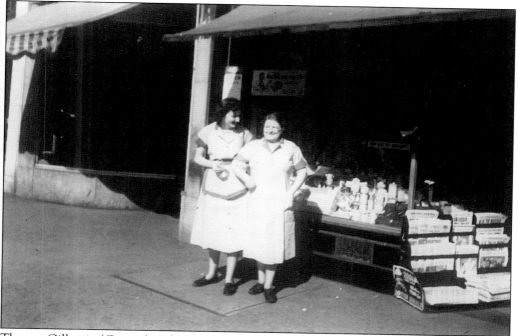

Theresa Gillespie (Ganem) and Doris Carter (right) both worked at Whalen's Drug Store on Congress Street.

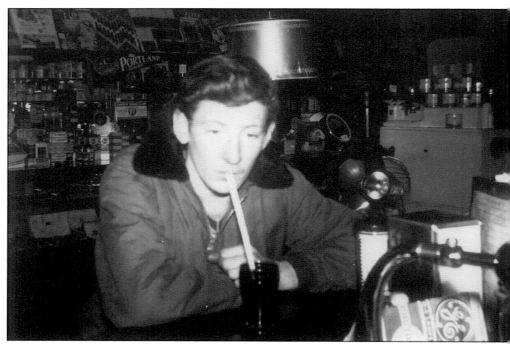

Remember the soda fountain? Ray Gillespie makes full use of the one at Whalen's Drug Store

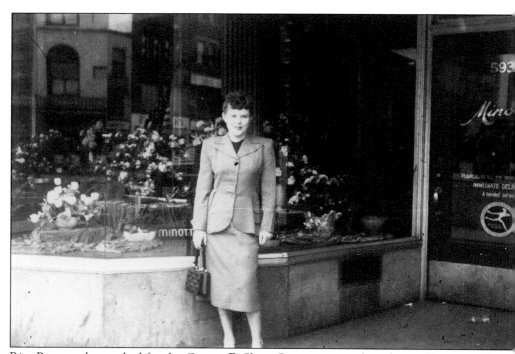

Rita Porter, who worked for the George E. Shaw Company, stands in front of Minott's Florist on Congress Street.

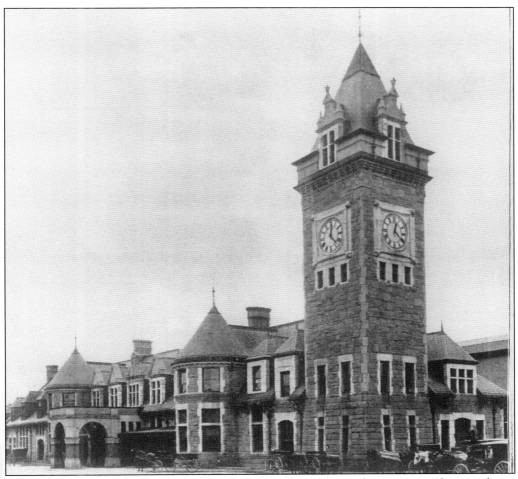

Union Station, a real landmark, was usually bustling as tourists and summer people poured into Maine and Portland in the 1950s. They brought a great deal of business to Congress Street. Will there ever be another passenger rail station in Portland? There is one sure thing—if it happens, it will be far smaller than the landmark, which, when it was razed, provided the greatest spur ever to the preservationist movement in Portland. Will it ever arise again from the ashes? And what of the fate of Congress Street?

Acknowledgments

My greatest thanks must go to Earle Shettleworth, executive director of the Maine Histori
Preservation Commission, and to Mrs. Catherine Carswell and her husband, Charles, for the
valiant efforts on my behalf for this Portland book. Earle's postcards and stereoscopic slide
provided a solid base from which to work, and Kitty Carswell gathered untouched material from
all over the city for me to use.

For the Jewish Community Center's pictures I'm indebted to Sumner T. Bernstein, for giving
me the first tip, and to Karen Lerman (JCC executive), Mrs. Evelyn Litman (JCC accountan
and a former co-worker with me on the Portland papers), and Dr. Jeffrey Finegold (chairman o
the JCC archives committee). Linda Aromson also gave me help with photographs as did Dea
Silverman.

Among those sources provided by Mrs. Carswell were Evelyn Sanborn Scribner, Mrs. A
Reali, Gerard Conley, Dana and Jean Childs, and Ruth Brown.

Key material came from Widgery Thomas Jr. (I'd like to belatedly thank Henry Thoma:
Widgery's cousin, for all the help he was on *Presque Isle, Caribou, and New Sweden*), Hartle
(Barney) Baxter II, and Bill Leavitt. Fred Thompson and Arthur Leavitt gave informatio
about the WCSH photograph, while Deborah Rumery was helpful just as she was on *August*
with pictures of the Gannett family. Betty Owen Jacoby, a member of my class at Wincheste
(Massachusetts) High School, even provided some Portland photographs.

John DiBiase, Gerald Davis, and Mike DiSimon gave information on the footbal
photographs.

I must apologize to three whom I thought I'd get in this book, but had enough pictures befor
I could get back to them: the Discatio family (though Mrs. Joseph Discatio is in the Nort
School photograph), Frank Collins of Parker's, and Mrs. Katherine Tolford of Congress Stree
Eyewear. Hopefully, we'll get out another Portland book if we sell the first print run of th
one.

Finally, I wish to thank the staff at Arcadia: Kirsty Sutton, who will be moving south soon a
the company continues its expansion, Jim Burkinshaw, Michael Guillory, and Aaron Faulkne
Never have so few done so much for so many.

Frank H. Sleepe